The Invent to Learn
Guide to the
micro:bit

Pauline Maas and Peter Heldens

Constructing Modern Knowledge Press

Editors: Gary Stager and Sylvia Libow Martinez

Cover and layout: Lindsay Balfour

Illustrations: Angelique Krijnen

All photos are credited to the authors unless otherwise noted.

ISBNs
Paperback: 978-1-955604-06-2
Hardcover: 978-1-955604-07-9

The micro:bit word mark, logo, and device belong to the micro:bit Educational Foundation. We have followed their convention of always using lowercase for the word micro:bit. MakeCode is a trademark of the Microsoft Corporation. All marks are the property of their respective owners.

9.4

While every precaution has been taken, the publisher and authors assume no responsibility for errors, omissions, changed information or URLs, or for damages resulting from the use of the information herein.

NOTE: Some of these projects call for tools and materials that can be dangerous if used improperly. Always follow manufacturer's guidelines, safety rules, and use common sense.

Praise for...
The Invent to Learn Guide to the micro:bit

"This book takes learners from the basics through complex programming challenges quickly with engaging projects and games. The authors do a terrific job of showing how micro:bits can be used by themselves, with external electronics like servos and LEDs, as well as to control online animations with Scratch. I am so excited for my students of all ages to play and learn with micro:bits using this book!"
—Kristin Burrus, Innovation Program Manager at the Global Center for Digital Innovation

"Thoughtfully scaffolded and bursting with creativity, *The Invent to Learn Guide to the micro:bit* is the guide to whimsical fun for which we have been waiting! Open-ended enough to encourage further exploration, you will feel confident and supported through each step of myriad projects. Whether you are new to the micro:bit or a seasoned programmer, your toolkit should include this wonderful guide!"
—Josh Burker, Educator and author of *The Invent to Learn Guide to Fun* and *The Invent to Learn Guide to More Fun*

"*The Invent to Learn Guide to the micro:bit* is a wonderful way to start using coding with intermediate and middle grade students. The colorful illustrations, creative ideas, and step-by-step instructions are sure to engage kids in hands-on learning experiences that build a foundation of coding skills beyond the limitations of an all-digital environment. I love the "phygital" approach to computational thinking that physical computing devices provide, and this book is a start-up guide appropriate for any class."
—Becky Keene, Microsoft Innovative Educator Expert

"Pauline came to our South African community and shared wonderful and imaginative micro:bit projects with our students. Now we have a book that will give young people around the world the chance to experience this joy as they master programming and technology with the micro:bit."
—Phuti Ragophala, "Techno Grannie" - Microsoft Innovative Educator Fellow

"This book is an essential part of every micro:bit educator's toolbox. There is quite literally something for everyone, no matter what they teach or how familiar they are with micro:bits. Filled with innovative and engaging ideas, the activities and projects in *The Invent to Learn Guide to the micro:bit* will grow with you and your students. Sample unit plans and the Design Canvas build computational thinking skills effortlessly with clear structures on how to plan projects for all learners."
—Sarah Rankin, Technology Coach, Anglophone School District South, Canada

"*The Invent to Learn Guide to the micro:bit* is the book novice and enthusiast micro:bit users have been waiting for. Colorful illustrations and resources throughout the book help guide readers in turning an idea into innovation. The authors did a brilliant job of combining basic materials with easy-to-follow physical computing examples that can be used throughout the year."
—Tonya Coats, Elementary Educator

"This is a well-written, tested, and thorough book that I can't wait to add to my library! Thank you Pauline for putting in the time and working with all of your student engineers and beta testers. This work is part of your ongoing community collaboration—you are an integral part of the micro:bit community making materials to keep students learning, building, and creating!"
—Melissa Wrenchey, Educator and Librarian, Tesla STEM High School, Washington

Contents

Preface

"Interdisciplinary projects in which the playful inclinations of children are leveraged to construct meaning."

This was one of the many sentences I highlighted in my dog-eared copy of *Invent to Learn: Making, Tinkering, and Engineering* when I read it back in 2016, saying "Yes! Yes! Yes!" to myself all the way through. It is not an overstatement to say that this book and the constructionist learning theory heavily influenced the creation of the MakeCode product at Microsoft in 2017. We wanted to create not just another code editor, but a tool that could combine the magic of making with the power of code in ways that lent themselves to self-expression and creativity. So, it is truly a crowning moment for us to now be featured in the latest version of *The Invent to Learn Guide to the micro:bit*!

I first knew of Pauline as @4pip on Twitter and immediately started following her and her amazing project posts. Then at a Microsoft Educator conference in Singapore, I was walking through the poster sessions, and saw a lady at the end of the row with flashy neopixel light shoes and micro:bit bracelets on her arms... it was Pauline, the micro:bit Queen! One of the many things I admire about Pauline is her ability to make things simple and delightful! Learning computer science doesn't have to be typing commands in a console window, it can be creating a Unicorn Greeting Card or a Wearable Flower LED badge.

Peter was introduced to me by a Microsoft colleague saying, "You need to meet this crazy Dutch guy! He's doing incredible things with the micro:bit," and sure enough, he was! I remember Peter showing me a video of his daughter who had attached a micro:bit to her field hockey stick and was using it to count the number of times she bounced her ball on the stick to automate her practice time. And since then, he's contributed many different projects to the MakeCode site including the ever-popular Milk Carton Robots.

Just as revolutionary as the Arduino was for democratizing physical computing in 2005, the micro:bit has brought it a step further and opened doors to classrooms and children around the world to play, tinker and make with hardware, electronics and code. And it's also opened doors to computing for many students who never saw themselves as technologists. The approach of combining a more holistic view of computer science—encompassing both hardware and software, and the pedagogy of "learning with your hands" has broadened the appeal of CS to many under-represented student populations. In a national survey in the UK, the BBC found a 70% increase in interest among girls to continue studying computing after having worked with the micro:bit. The popularity of the micro:bit is a testament to its ability to engage learners of all types—the micro:bit is now available in over 70 countries around the world with millions of students creating and coding with it every month from Sri Lanka to Uruguay.

The projects created by Pauline and Peter make *The Invent to Learn Guide to the micro:bit* an invaluable resource for educators, students, parents, or anyone who wants to learn more about the creative possibilities of the micro:bit.

Happy Making and Coding!

Jacqueline Russell

Product Manager, Microsoft MakeCode

Introducing the micro:bit

The micro:bit is a small computer designed for young people and students to learn how to code and make interactive projects. In 2015 1.3 million kids in the UK were given a micro:bit. By 2020, kids in more than sixty countries had access to this tiny, but powerful single board computer.

You can code the micro:bit with many different programming languages, including MakeCode, Scratch, JavaScript, MicroPython, and the micro:bit MakeCode phone app.

The micro:bit features sensors, LED lights, and connections that can control motors and other peripherals. micro:bits can also communicate with each other via radio. The fun starts when you connect a small battery pack and bring your dream projects to life.

What's on the micro:bit?

The micro:bit has built-in sensors for inputs (buttons, motion, temperature, light, and compass) and outputs (25 small LED lights). It also has the ability to communicate via Bluetooth or radio. The latest micro:bit (version 2) also contains a speaker, microphone, and can detect touch.

Each micro:bit talks to the world with 25 external connections along the bottom edge of the board, called "pins." Five of these pins are larger to make connections easier. These pins are labeled 0, 1, 2, 3V, and GND. The projects in this book will use these five pins to connect external devices like buttons, LEDs, servo motors, buzzers, and more.

P0	Pin 0	Used for input and output, speaker connection
P1	Pin 1	Used for input and output
P2	Pin 2	Used for input and output
3V	Power	Any external device needing three volts can connect to this pin.
GND	Ground	Any external device in a circuit will use this pin to complete the circuit.

Front

USB connector

25 LEDs

Button A

Pins

Back

Reset button   Battery connector

Button B

MakeCode Tour

Most of the projects in this book are programmed using the MakeCode programming language with a micro:bit connected to a computer. The software runs in most up-to-date browsers like Chrome. That means you have access to your programs anywhere, anytime. MakeCode is block-based, making it easy to learn and use. MakeCode can also translate your blocks into JavaScript or Python. Programs created in MakeCode are downloaded or saved to the micro:bit as if the micro:bit was a USB drive connected to your computer. MakeCode is free to use and works in lots of different human languages. All of these features make MakeCode and the micro:bit a popular team for coding and physical computing.

Open Chrome to makecode.microbit.org. Select **New Project** and the interface screen for MakeCode will open. The three main areas are:

- The **Workspace** where you assemble your program
- The **Toolbox** where you find blocks to assemble your program
- The **Simulator** where you can preview how your program will run on a micro:bit.

Other features of MakeCode will be introduced as we build projects with the micro:bit and MakeCode.

Watch an introductory video about the micro:bit at microbit.inventtolearn.com.

Warm Ups

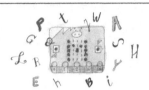

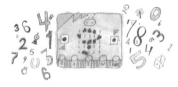
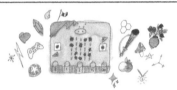

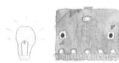

Start with a Heart

In this project, you will learn how to download your code to the micro:bit.

Programming

- Go to makecode.com
- Select micro:bit as the device you wish to program
- Start a new project by clicking on **New Project** under **My Projects**
- Name your project *Heart* and click **Create**
- Build the program as shown

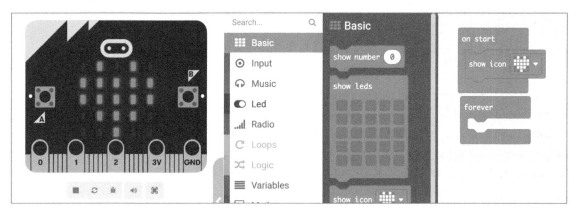

Understanding the code

Write a program for the micro:bit by dragging blocks out of the Toolbox and onto the Workspace.

This program displays a heart icon. Drag the `show icon` block out of the **Basic** section of the Toolbox and place it inside the `on start` block. The default icon is the heart. If you do not see the heart icon on the Simulator on the left side of the MakeCode screen, something is wrong. Try again!

The Simulator shows a preview of your program, but the code is not running on the micro:bit... yet. Every time you write a new program, or change your program, you must download the code to the micro:bit.

Pair for an easy one-click download to the micro:bit

MakeCode makes downloading a program to the micro:bit as simple as saving a file. To use this feature, your micro:bit needs to be paired with MakeCode on the computer you are using. Pairing creates a handshake through which your code travels from the computer to the micro:bit.

Once the micro:bit and computer are paired, clicking the **Download** button in MakeCode puts the current version of your code on the micro:bit. The current version of your project saves on the MakeCode website.

- Connect your micro:bit to the computer with a USB cable
- Click on the three dots next to the **Download** button
- Select **Connect device**
- Follow the directions in the message windows and click on the unique name or number of your micro:bit
- Select **Connect**
- Click on the **Download** button to send your code to the micro:bit

Your program begins running as soon as it is downloaded to the micro:bit.

You should see a heart icon appear on your micro:bit. If a heart does not appear, something went wrong! Try again.

You only have to pair the micro:bit to your computer once. The next time you connect the micro:bit, MakeCode should remember the unique name of your micro:bit and pair automatically. This assumes you are using the same micro:bit and the same computer. In classroom settings, this may not be the case and you will need to pair the devices again. If this download method is not working, try the two-step download found in the Tips at the end of this *Warm Up* section.

Tips
- Pairing only works with the latest versions of Google Chrome and Microsoft Edge browsers, and a micro:bit with the latest firmware. See more about these requirements at makecode.microbit.org/device/usb/webusb
- Be aware that versions of your code are not saved on your computer when you use the pairing method. If you wish to save versions as you work on a project, click on the **Save** button at the bottom of the MakeCode screen and then the **Download** button to make sure a version is saved on your hard drive and also downloaded to the micro:bit.
- Chromebook users must enable the USB ports.
- Throughout this book, code, templates, videos, and other resources can be found online at microbit.inventtolearn.com.

Name Badge

In this project, you will display your name and a number on the micro:bit.

Programming

- Go to makecode.com
- Select micro:bit as the device you wish to program
- Start a new project by clicking on **New Project** under **My Projects**
- Name your project *Name Badge*, and click **Create**

All of the things MakeCode knows how to do can be found in blocks stored in the Toolbox in the middle of the screen. As the programmer, you solve problems by putting the blocks together in many ways.

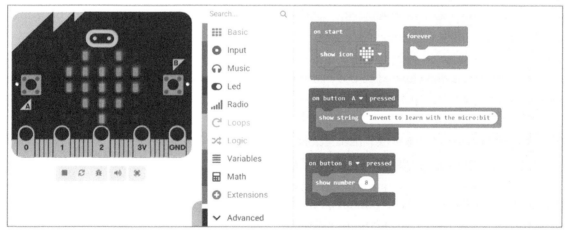

Drag a block out of the Toolbox to the Workspace on the right-hand side of the screen and assemble them into a stack. The bumps and indents of the blocks help them snap together like puzzle pieces.

You can have multiple stacks of blocks in the Workspace. All the blocks in the Workspace are considered one program and will be downloaded to the micro:bit together.

Each kind of block is stored in a different color-coded category. You don't need to memorize where blocks are stored since you can just click on the color you are looking for and the find the block in that section of the Toolbox.

Be sure to connect all of your blocks together. You should hear a faint click as the blocks connect. The order in which you create stacks of interconnected blocks does not matter.

- Build the program as shown
- A little arrow in a block lets you choose different actions. Click on the arrow to see the choices. A white circle means you can type in it.
- Click on the A or B buttons on the micro:bit Simulator on the left-hand side of the screen to see how your program will run once it is downloaded to the micro:bit.
- Connect your micro:bit to the computer
- Pair your micro:bit to the MakeCode website if you haven't done so already
- Download your code to the micro:bit

Understanding the code

Write programs for the micro:bit by dragging blocks out of the Toolbox and onto the Workspace. Blocks that respond to inputs, like buttons, have no bumps or indentations on their top or bottom and are called **event blocks**, since they run when an event happens. The lack of bumps signals that these blocks stand on their own and cannot be connected to other stacks of blocks. `on start`, `forever`, and `on button pressed` are all examples of event blocks. When the event happens, all the blocks contained inside the C shape run one at a time, from top to bottom.

When the micro:bit is powered on with the new program loaded, the first thing it does is run the blocks contained inside the `on start` block. In this case, it displays the heart icon. You choose the icon shape by clicking on the pop-up menu on the block. If you do not see the heart icon on the micro:bit display, the program was not properly downloaded to the micro:bit. Try again!

When a program includes an `on start` block, any instructions contained within will run automatically as soon as your program is downloaded to the micro:bit, but only once. The next time your micro:bit is powered, either by connecting it to the battery box or the computer, it will run those instructions once again since it remembers the last program stored on it.

The `on button pressed` block runs a list of instructions whenever the specified button on the micro:bit is pressed. We programmed instructions for both the A and B buttons in this project.

Information that changes in a computer program is called a variable. The two primary kinds of variables used by MakeCode are strings and numbers. Numbers are self-explanatory and used in calculations. Strings are letters, words, or combinations of words.

When the A button is pressed, it runs the block `show string`. You enter text into the white area of the block, and MakeCode automatically adds quote marks around the text to remind you that it is a string. When the program is downloaded to the micro:bit, the text will scroll on the micro:bit display.

When the B button is pressed, a number will be displayed.

Changing the program in the micro:bit

The micro:bit holds one program at a time. If you make changes to your program in MakeCode, you must download the new code to the micro:bit to see it run. You will do this often while programming the micro:bit. Try changing your program and download the new version to the micro:bit. See how the new code replaces the old program?

Challenges

- Have the micro:bit display: *Hello, my name is* (your name)
- Choose another icon for the `on start` instruction
- Try displaying different numbers when button B is pressed
- Show something (a number or a string) when both the A+B buttons are pressed
- See if you can have the micro:bit perform some arithmetic by inserting plus, minus, multiply or divide in the input where a number goes. Hint: Find the round arithmetic block you want to use in the **Math** section of the Toolbox.

Tips

- Blocks fit together like pieces in a jigsaw puzzle. You can hear it and see it when they snap into place. If they do not snap together, your program will not run properly.
- You can delete a block or stack of blocks using the delete key, a right mouse click (Windows), CTRL-click (Mac), or dragging it back to the Toolbox where a trash bin will appear.

 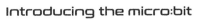

Make an Animation

Create an animation to display on the micro:bit!

Programming

- Go to makecode.com
- Start a new project and name it *Animation*
- Recreate the program in your MakeCode Workspace
- Test your program in the Simulator
- Connect your micro:bit to the computer
- Download your code to the micro:bit
- Press the A button. Does your animation work?

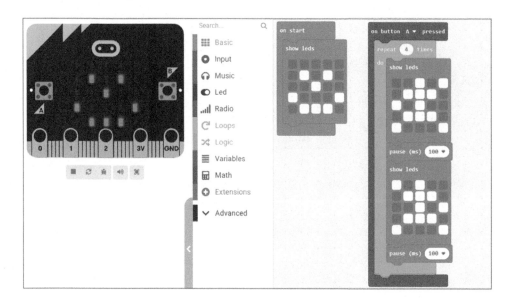

Understanding the code

This project introduces three new blocks: `show leds`, `pause`, and `repeat`.

Each of the LEDs on the micro:bit display is a pixel just like a pixel on your TV or computer screen. The micro:bit display has 25 pixels, in five rows of five. By comparison, a 32" inch TV has 1920 pixels in each of 1080 rows (2,073,600 pixels total). When a combination of pixels are turned on and off, they create pictures.

The `show leds` block allows you to turn on or off the pixels on the micro:bit display by clicking on them.

`pause` causes your program to wait for a specific number of milliseconds. There are 1,000 milliseconds in one second. So, 100 ms equals 1/10th of a second. How long should your pause be if you want your program to pause for half a second?

`repeat` tells the sequence of instructions within it to repeat a specific number of times. In this case, you will repeat them four times, but you can change that number and watch what happens.

When the A button is pressed, a flipbook-style animation will be displayed on the micro:bit. This is achieved by flipping back and forth between two shapes with a pause in between.

The pause is important because computers run faster than humans perceive change. If there was no pause, you may not see the shapes change. When people write commercial software like video games, speed is key. Each instruction the computer executes takes time, even if it is just tiny fraction of one second. We don't have to worry about efficiency now, we just want to make the animation look good.

Tips

- To save your project, click the Save icon next to the program name.
- To start a new project, click on Home at the top left of the screen.
- When you click on Home, you will also see all of your previously saved projects. Click on any of them to reload it to MakeCode. Then you can download that program to your micro:bit or use it as the starting point for a new similar project.

Challenges

- Make the animation run more times by changing the input to the `repeat` block.
- Experiment with the pause duration by trying different numbers. If you want the animation to look smooth and steady, choose the same number for both pauses. This is a common programming technique.
- Add a third or fourth shape to your animation (perhaps you can create a dancing stick figure). Don't forget to pause in between showing each icon.

Lucky Number

Shake the micro:bit and display a lucky number!

Programming

- Go to makecode.com
- Start a new project and name it *Lucky Number*
- Create the program in the MakeCode Workspace
- Test your program in the MakeCode Simulator
- Connect your micro:bit to the computer
- Download your code to the micro:bit
- Shake the micro:bit and see what happens! If you don't see a number displayed, check your program, your connection, and download the program again.

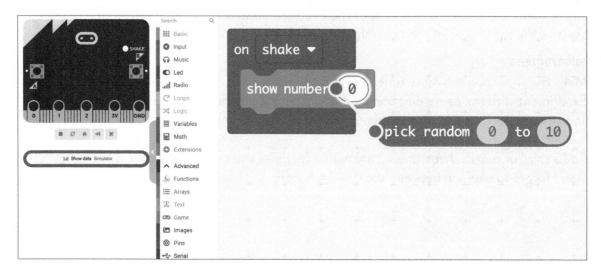

The Invent to Learn Guide to the micro:bit

Understanding the code

Your program will generate a random number between 0 and 10 and display that value.

Drag the `pick random` reporter block from the **Math** Toolbox into the empty hole in the `show number` block. This may take a bit of practice. Drag the `pick random` block until its middle is over the number in the `show number` block and it should snap right into place. You will see a yellow outline and red dots to help you line up the blocks.

Reporter blocks are round or hexagonal blocks that can be moved into the inputs of other blocks. They "report" numbers or other results to the blocks they are inserted in.

Be sure to type a 0 and 10 into the `pick random` block.

`on shake` works like `on button` except it waits for a user to shake the micro:bit before running the series of instructions.

Tips

- One way to find a block you're looking for is to type its name in the search box at the top of the Toolbox.
- When you download your program to the micro:bit you should see a small light flickering on the micro:bit near the USB connector.

Challenges

- Change the program to simulate flipping a coin
- Change the program to simulate rolling a die

Your First Game

This project creates a very simple handheld game.

Programming

- Go to makecode.com
- Start a new project and name it *Game*
- Create the program in the Workspace
- Test your program in the Simulator
- Connect your micro:bit to the computer
- Download your code to the micro:bit
- Play the game!

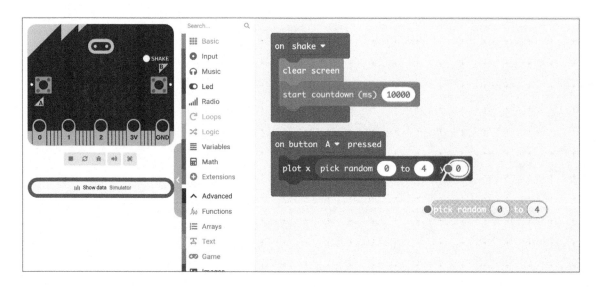

Understanding the code

The `plot x y` block found in the **Led** Toolbox turns on an LED on the micro:bit display at the location (X , Y).

The top left-hand LED is (0 , 0).

The bottom right-hand LED is (4 , 4)

The X axis is horizontal (left-to-right).

The Y axis is vertical (top-to-bottom).

Using the `pick random` blocks as the X and Y values in the `plot x y` block will light the LEDs randomly. Be sure to drag two `pick random` blocks into the values for both X and Y.

Picking a random number between 0 and 4 for both X and Y ensures that one of the 25 LED positions on the micro:bit display will be selected to turn on.

The `start countdown` block is found in the **Game** panel, under **Advanced**.

Tips

- If you mouse over an LED in the Simulator, MakeCode will remind you of its coordinates.
- Click on **Advanced** to show more blocks that are normally reserved for super-duper programmers. It's generally a good idea to avoid the blocks found under **Advanced** unless a project requires them. In this game, it's handy to use the `start countdown` block because it automatically keeps track of a countdown timer and end of game.

Playing the game

When you shake the micro:bit, a countdown of 10,000 milliseconds (10 seconds) begins.

Press the A button as quickly as possible to light up as many LEDs as you can before time runs out.

When the timer runs out, the lit LEDs will turn off and *Game Over* will be displayed. A score of zero will be shown. This simple game does not keep score. Future projects will.

Challenges

- Play against a friend by downloading this game on two micro:bits
- Change the countdown so a less experienced gamer can play the game
- If you have a micro:bit V2, add sound effect to indicate "game over"

What's the Temperature?

There is a temperature sensor built into the micro:bit. You can build a digital thermometer or use the temperature reading to control some other behavior in more elaborate projects. Imagine building a climate-controlled greenhouse or pet habitat.

Programming

- Go to makecode.com
- Start a new project and name it *Thermometer*
- Create the program in the MakeCode Workspace
- The value displayed as the current temperature in the Simulator will not be accurate. The Simulator is not reading the actual micro:bit temperature sensor.
- Connect your micro:bit to the computer
- Download your code to the micro:bit
- Observe the displayed temperature on the micro:bit.

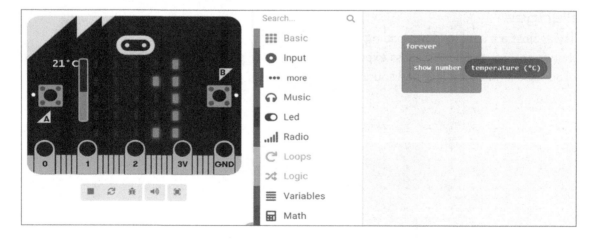

Understanding the code

The `forever` block causes a sequence of instructions to run over and over again *forever*. It runs automatically when the micro:bit is powered.

In this program, we will use a `temperature` sensor block from the **Input** section of the Toolbox to make `show number` display the current temperature in degrees Celsius.

Since that value will be displayed forever in a loop, changes in temperature will appear on the micro:bit display.

Things to Try

- Put the micro:bit in the refrigerator
- Place the micro:bit between your hands
- Blow on your micro:bit to make the temperature rise
- Connect the battery box and measure the temperature outside

Tips

- The temperature sensor is on the back of the micro:bit and does not register changes in temperature as quickly as you might think, so be patient.
- Do not get the micro:bit wet! Do not take it in the rain! Do not submerge it in water, ice, or snow! It might be possible to place the micro:bit and battery box in a waterproof container, like a Ziploc bag if you need it to measure the temperature of liquids, but first ask an adult for permission.

Challenges

- Program the micro:bit to display the temperature in Fahrenheit. Hint: You are going to have to perform a mathematical calculation on the temperature value.
- Change the program to show the temperature only when a button is pressed, rather than continuously.

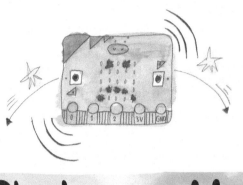

Shake it Up

The micro:bit has a built-in accelerometer. That's a sensor that detects movement. It can react to being tilted, shaken, turned over, or dropped (carefully). In this project, we will write a program that reacts to being shaken with different levels of force.

Programming

- Go to makecode.com
- Start a new project and name it *Shake*
- Create the program as shown in the MakeCode Workspace
- Click on each `on shake` block to change the events to `3g`, `6g`, and `8g`
- Choose an icon in each event block to display when a different level of force is used to shake the micro:bit. Be creative!
- Connect your micro:bit to the computer
- Download your code to the micro:bit
- Shake your micro:bit hard, and then harder to see the icons change

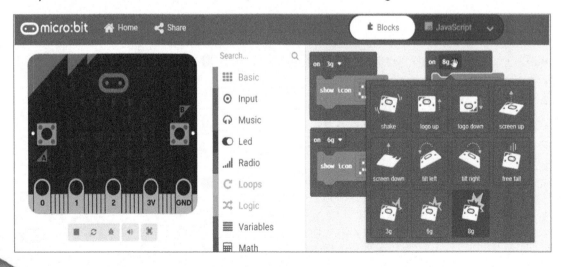

The Invent to Learn Guide to the micro:bit

Understanding the code

The `on shake` block may be changed to react to other accelerometer triggers. In this case, we are using 3g, 6g, and 8g as our events.

The *g* represents gravitational force. 1g is the equivalent of the normal gravitational force on earth. 3g is three times that force, 6g is six times that force, etc. So, shaking the micro:bit harder should make your program display different graphics.

8g is the maximum gravitational acceleration that can be measured by the micro:bit.

Tips

- The Simulator cannot be used to simulate 3g, 6g, or 8g shakes. It does not know what's actually happening to the micro:bit.
- Don't be too rough or you might break the micro:bit

Challenges

- Experiment with your program and change the on 3g, 6g, or 8g to free fall, tilt left or tilt right, logo up or logo down, screen up or screen down. What happens?
- If you use free fall, make sure your micro:bit will land on something soft (like a cushion or grass)
- Instead of displaying an icon, can you make one or more of your events display some text?
- Can you play an animation when a user exerts a lot of force?

micro:bit Tips

micro:bit unplugged

When your micro:bit is connected to your computer via a USB cable, it gets power from the computer. To run your micro:bit independently (untethered), connect a battery pack to the micro:bit battery socket. Once batteries are connected, your program will run on the micro:bit. The micro:bit remembers your program even when you turn it off and runs the program again once reconnected to a power source. Learn more about micro:bit battery and power options in *micro:bit Power Possibilities* in the *Resources* section of this book.

Two-step download (The classic way)

If for some reason pairing isn't working with your computer, there is another way to download code to the micro:bit. This method requires two steps: save the program file to the computer, and then copy the program file to the micro:bit.

- Connect your micro:bit to the computer with a USB cable
- Click the **Download** button to save the file to your computer
- A screen will appear that your download is complete
- Go to your Downloads folder and drag the .hex file to your micro:bit. The micro:bit will appear in your list of drives, similar to a USB drive. You can also copy and paste the file to the micro:bit.

Your program begins running as soon as it is downloaded to the micro:bit.

You may need to update the micro:bit firmware

Firmware is like the operating system of the micro:bit. It is updated from time to time. If your micro:bit is not running the current firmware, MakeCode may not function properly.

- If you try to pair your micro:bit and your firmware is not up to date, you will see an error message
- Click on **Check Firmware**.
- Follow the instructions to download and install the latest firmware.

What's New V2?

In late 2020, a new micro:bit was released. The new micro:bit (Version 2 or V2) includes an on-board speaker and a couple of new sensors. These new sensors—the logo and the microphone—provide additional ways to interact with the micro:bit. It also has a faster processor and more memory to hold bigger programs.

The on-board speaker lets you play tones without attaching a speaker or headphones.

The microphone detects changes in noise level. Make a loud or soft sound and you can trigger something to happen, much in the same way that pressing a button does.

The logo is the little oval-shaped picture found above the LED display. Touching it closes an electrical circuit and sends that news to the brain of the micro:bit, its microprocessor.

In order to use these new features in micro:bit projects, MakeCode added some new blocks to the Toolbox.

In the **Input** section of the Toolbox, you will see blocks specifically for programming the micro:bit V2. These blocks appear at the bottom of the palette under the heading micro:bit (V2). Only micro:bit V2 boards will understand programs using these blocks When you use these blocks, you will see a small V2 logo in the Simulator above the GND pin.

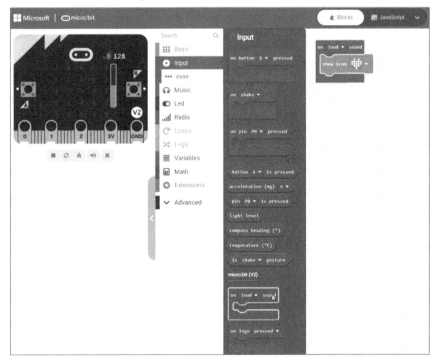

The `on sound` event block is triggered when the microphone hears a sound. You can select if it responds to loud or quiet sounds. When it does, the rest of the instructions inside that container block are run.

The `on logo` block waits until someone touches the logo on the micro:bit and then responds accordingly. This block can sense four different conditions:

- The logo is pressed
- The logo is touched (quicker than a press)
- The logo is released (your finger comes off the logo)
- The logo is long pressed (held down)

The new `on logo` and `on sound` blocks behave just like the `on button` or `on shake` blocks. They run continuously waiting to sense something and then take action by running the blocks inside of them.

There is also a new `play sound` block in the **Music** section of the Toolbox that uses the on-board speaker of the micro:bit V2 to play fun sounds.

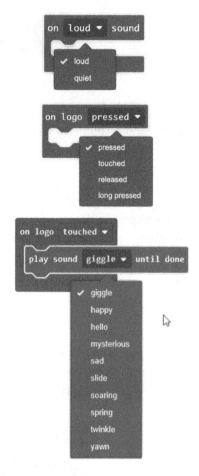

If you have a micro:bit V1

An original micro:bit (V1) will still work with MakeCode, as long as you don't use the special V2 blocks. Using V2 blocks in a program on a micro:bit V1 will generate a "Incompatible Code" warning during download and cause a 927 error code to scroll across the micro:bit display.

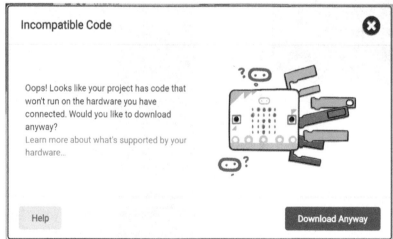

micro:bit V1	micro:bit V2
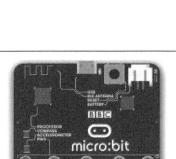	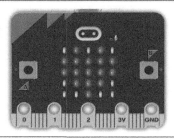
• Programmable buttons A and B • 25 LED Lights • 3 large input/output pins • 1 3V pin • 1 GND pin • 20 small input/output pins • Light sensor (using LEDs)	• Programmable buttons A and B • 25 LED Lights • 3 large input/output pins • 1 3V pin • 1 GND pin • 20 small input/output pins • Light sensor (using LEDs) • **Touch sensor (using logo)** • **Sound sensor** • **Notched pin connectors for more secure connections**

• Bluetooth 4.0 • Radio • Temperature sensor • Accelerometer • Compass • Battery socket • USB connection • Reset button • Memory - 256kB Flash, 16kB RAM	• Bluetooth 5.0 • Radio • Temperature sensor • Accelerometer • Compass • Battery socket • USB connection • Reset button • Memory - 512kB Flash, 128kB RAM • **Speaker** • **Microphone** • **Power indicator LED** • **On/off button (reset button - press & hold to sleep, press to wake)**

Getting Started

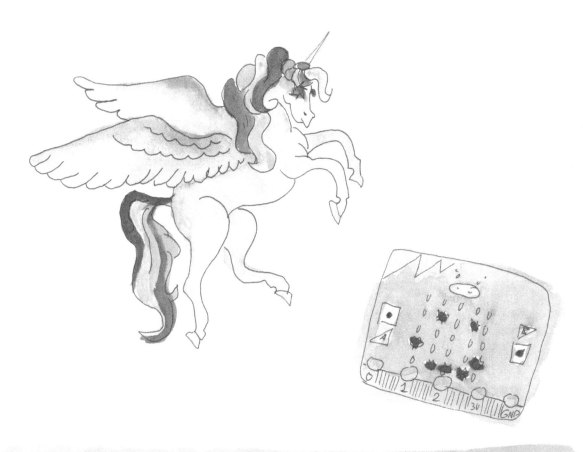

Unicorn Greeting Card

Make a Unicorn greeting card with a flashing LED light. You can use the Unicorn template or draw your own picture. In this project, we will attach an external LED to the micro:bit and write code to make it blink. Once you successfully control one LED, you might try two or three.

Materials
micro:bit, USB cable & battery pack, 2 alligator clips, 1 LED light, scissors & markers, construction paper or cardstock, aluminum foil, tape, Unicorn template.

Make

1. Assemble your materials.

2. Cut out your unicorn and color it. Glue or tape on the construction paper.

3. Test your LED light by connecting it to a powered micro:bit. Touch the long leg to where the micro:bit says 3V and the short leg on GND.

4. Press your LED light through the paper, making sure you remember where the long (positive) and short (negative or ground) legs are.

5. Use a pen or marker to label the positive and negative legs of the LED.

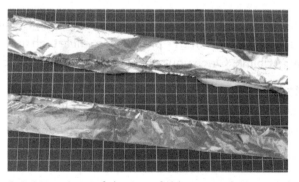

6. Cut two pieces of aluminum foil, long enough to cover the construction paper. Fold your aluminum foil a few times to make it stronger.

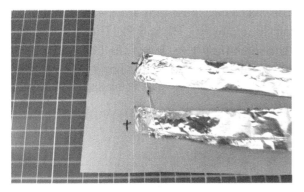

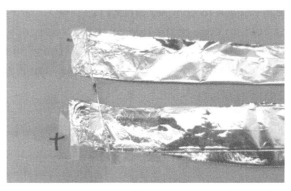

7. Put the foil under the legs of the LED. Press the legs into the aluminum foil. Make sure that the foil strips do not touch each other! (That would cause a short circuit.)

8. Attach each leg to the foil "wires" with tape. Make the connection as sturdy as possible.

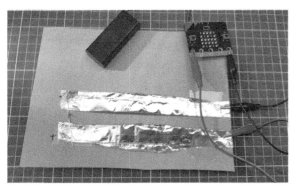

9. Cut the other end of the aluminum foil strips at the edge of the card. Attach one alligator clip to each aluminum strip.

Connect the alligator clip connected to the positive leg of the LED to the large hole P0 on the micro:bit and the other alligator clip to the large hole GND.

10. Download the code to the micro:bit and test it out.

Congratulations! You made a flashing card!

Template

Use the *Unicorn Greeting Card* template or make your own. Find this downloadable template file at microbit.inventtolearn.com.

Connections

You can choose to connect an LED to pin 0, 1 or P2 on the micro:bit. These pins are the large holes at the bottom edge of the micro:bit. As a shortcut, we call these pins P0, P1, and P2. The long leg (positive) of the LED connects to one of those pins and the short (negative) leg of the LED must connect to the ground (GND) pin. In this example, the long leg of the LED is connected to pin 0 (P0).

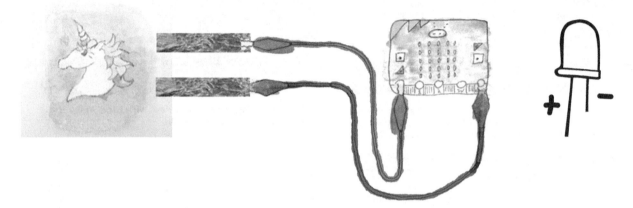

Tips

- Test your LED before assembling the card. It might be possible that the LED is dead. Do this by connecting the long leg of the LED to the 3V pin and the short leg to the GND pin on a powered micro:bit. The 3V pin is always powered on.
- Connecting the alligator clip to the hole ensures a good connection.
- You can connect the positive leg of an LED to 0, 1, or 2 as long as you change the code to match. The negative leg must always connect to GND. Make sure to select the same pin for the connection and the code.

Programming

The code for the unicorn is simple. Turn the LED on, turn the LED off, and repeat the entire process four times. Along with flashing the LED, add an animation to the micro:bit display.

- Create a new project and name it *Unicorn*
- Create the program
- Read the program and predict what it does
- Test your program with the Simulator
- Connect the micro:bit
- Download the new code to the micro:bit
- Test the new program on the micro:bit

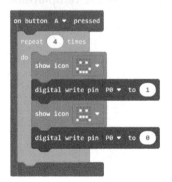

Understanding the code

When the program starts, show a space creature icon on the micro:bit display.

When the A button is pressed on the micro:bit, repeat the list of instructions inside the `repeat` block 4 times.

Show an icon of a happy face on the micro:bit's display.

`digital write pin` is a command that tells the micro:bit to send electricity to an output pin you specify. You select the pin where your LED is connected, in this case P0, and then "write" a value to it, in this case 1. Writing a value of 1 to a pin indicates it should turn on. Sometimes, this is referred to setting the pin "high." The `digital write pin` block is found in the **Pins** section in the **Advanced** group of the Toolbox.

Next, show the sad face icon and turn the LED off by setting the value of P0 to 0.

Download the program to your micro:bit and press the A button to see if the program works as planned. If not, check the code and your connections and see what you did wrong.

Tips

- If you want the flashing to slow down, add a pause.
- If you get tired of dragging blocks out of the Toolbox, you may copy one already found on your Workspace. Simply right-click (Windows) or Control-click (Mac) on a block and choose **Duplicate**. Then drag the new copy where you want it. You may also select a block by clicking on it and using standard copy and paste keyboard commands.

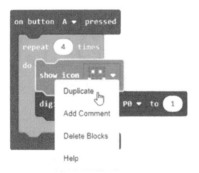

Challenges

- Change the speed of the LED flashing
- Make a four-icon animation on the micro:bit and make the LED turn on or off with each icon change
- Program some magic to occur when the B button is pressed
- Add more LEDs to your card
- Design a new card from scratch

JingLe BeLLs

MakeCode lets you program a micro:bit to play music. In this project, we will experiment with various ways to play notes, familiar melodies, or compose your own tune. Since the micro:bit V1 does not have its own speaker, you will need to connect headphones, earphones, or a speaker.

Materials
micro:bit, USB cable & battery pack, 2 alligator clips, piezo speaker or earphones.

Note: This build is not necessary if you are using a micro:bit V2 since it has a built-in speaker.

Make

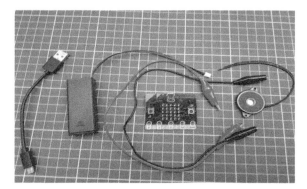

1. Assemble your materials.

2. Attach alligator clips to pins P0 and GND of the micro:bit.

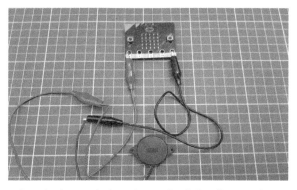

3. (speaker) Attach the other ends of the alligator clips to the piezo speaker.

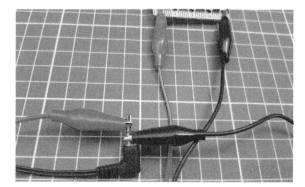

3. (earphones) Attach the other ends of the alligator clips to the earphone plug as shown.

Connections

MakeCode **Music** blocks only send signals to the P0 pin. You must connect your speaker or headphones to P0 and GND. Note: The colors of cables are not important.

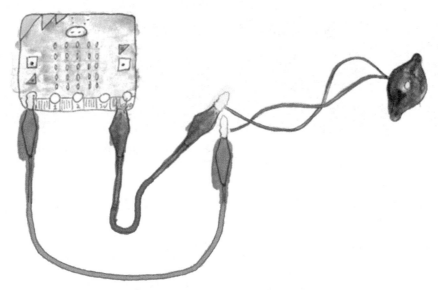

Piezo speaker connections

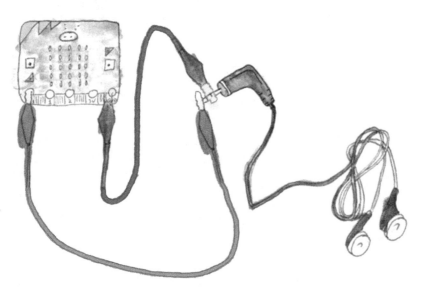

Earphone connections

Programming - Music making

MakeCode includes several ways to generate tones and play melodies.

Create the following program. The micro:bit will make music when you press either or both of its buttons. When you click in the white oval in the `play tone` block, a piano keyboard pops up allowing you to choose a note by clicking on it.

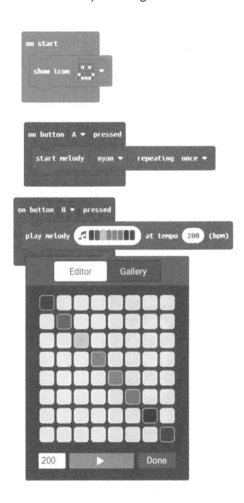

- Create a new project and name it *Music*
- Reproduce the program
- Read the program
- Predict what it does
- Test your program with the Simulator
- Connect the micro:bit to your computer and either a speaker or earphones
- Download the new code to the micro:bit
- Test the new program on the micro:bit and amaze your friends with your musical talent

Understanding the code - Music making

There are lots of ways to make music in MakeCode. The best way to understand the different blocks in the **Music** panel of the Toolbox is to experiment with them.

The `play tone` block generates a single musical note. The note is selected on the built-in piano keyboard or by entering the frequency you wish to play. The length of the note is measured as a beat, a multiple of a beat, or fraction of a beat. You can assemble these blocks to compose an entire melody.

Challenges

- Compose a new melody in the Editor of the `play melody` block inside `on button B pressed`
- Change the tempo in beats per minute (bpm)
- Try selecting one of the melodies in the Gallery of the `play melody` block.
- The `start melody` and `play melody` blocks are different. How do they work? What is the difference?

Programming - Jingle Bells

You can also program the micro:bit to play a melody translated from sheet music. Jingle Bells is a simple and familiar melody to teach the micro:bit. Use the color-coded Editor in the `play melody` block to compose melodic phrases. Those phrases will be assembled like musical building blocks to form the Jingle Bells melody.

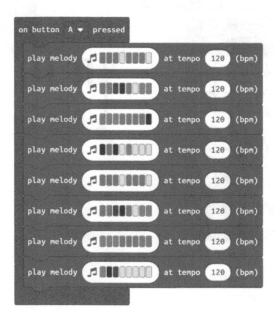

Jingle Bells
James Lord Pierpont

- Create a new project and name it *Jingle Bells*
- Copy the program
- Read the program and try to predict what it does
- Test your program with the Simulator
- Connect the micro:bit to your computer and either a speaker or earphones
- Download the new code to the micro:bit
- Test the new program on the micro:bit and annoy your friends

Understanding the code - Jingle Bells

The `on start` block causes a simple animation to play. This is a good way to make sure that everything is working when you power your micro:bit. A good debugging strategy is to change the animation slightly while debugging a project to make sure that the program downloaded properly to the micro:bit.

When the A button is pressed, a series of short melodic fragments will play in order to recreate Jingle Bells. If you hit a clunker, change the program.

If you wish to compose a more complex melody, use a series of `play tone` blocks combined with rest blocks.

Tips

- The piezo speaker or earphone must always be connected to pin P0 and GND.
- The play tone block can use a musical note from the piano keyboard as its pitch value or the actual frequency, measured in Hertz (Hz), to experiment with pitches between notes.

Challenges

- Can you play a new song composed of `play tone` blocks?
- Try to create an animation to accompany a melody being played.
- Explain what is happening in this code.
- Insert a `set tempo` block into a program before notes are played. What happens if you change the bpm value?
- Can you write a program to make music out of randomly generated notes or durations or both?
- Try using different volumes in your song.

Turkey Trot

Make everyone's favorite paper turkey come alive! You can even add music or a remote control.

Materials

micro:bit, USB cable & battery pack, 3 alligator to male jumper cables, small 180-degree 3-volt servo motor, construction paper, cardboard box, 2 clothespins, hot glue gun, googly eyes, markers, tape, Turkey template.

Make

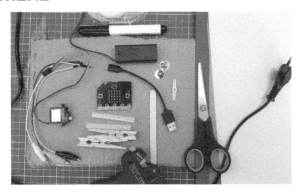

1. Gather your materials.

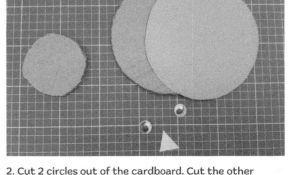

2. Cut 2 circles out of the cardboard. Cut the other pieces of the turkey out of colorful construction paper.

3. Glue the turkey's face and eyes on one cardboard circle to make a head. Of course, you also can draw the face if you wish or don't have cool googly eyes.

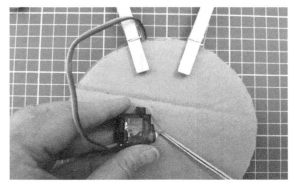

4. Make a hole in the bigger cardboard circle large enough to poke through the small turning wheel of your servo motor.

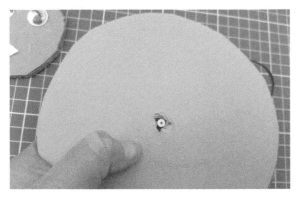

5. Put the white gear on the small hub of the servomotor. Turn it by hand to make sure it turns easily.

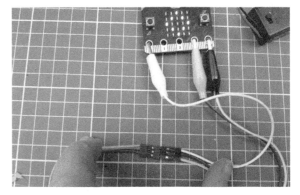

6. Program your micro:bit and attach the servo according to the Connections diagram. Make sure that all the cables are attached properly.

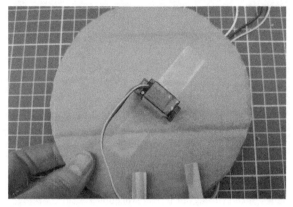

7. Tape the servo on the back of the big circle. If you don't do this, your servo will also turn.

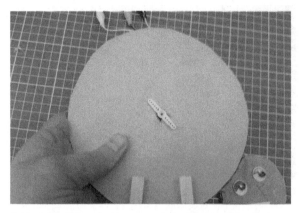

8. Turn the large circle over and glue the small turkey head on the small white blade that comes with most servos. Try the motor to see if the head moves.

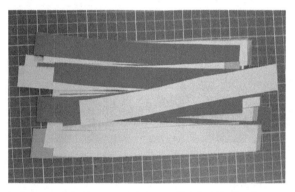

9. Cut construction paper into small strips for feathers. Glue or tape the ends together to make loops.

10 Glue the feathers onto the big circle. Your turkey is now ready. If you have another idea to decorate your turkey, go for it!

Template

Use the *Turkey Trot* template or make your own. Find this downloadable template file at microbit.inventtolearn.com.

Connections

Connecting a servo to the micro:bit can be a bit tricky. Servos have three wires that control their movement. One wire is where the servo gets power and one wire must connect to ground to complete the circuit. The third wire is how the servo gets its "instructions" from the micro:bit. This third wire can connect to P0, P1, or P2. We will use P0 in this example.

Usually, you can tell the three wires apart, but this might take a bit of debugging since different servos label their wires with different color schemes. These color assignments are common.

- Brown or black to GND
- Red to 3V
- Yellow or orange to P0 to get instructions

Many servos come with the wires ending in a "female" connector that is commonly used to connect servos. To connect your servo to your micro:bit, you either need to use three alligator clips with a male header wire to make the connections easy, or you can use standard alligator clips with short pieces of solid jumper wire (commonly found in craft or electronics projects). Each of these short pieces of wire may be inserted into the servo connector and connected to an alligator clip connected to the micro:bit. The color of the alligator clips and wire do not matter as long as the pins on the micro:bit connect properly to the servo connector.

When properly connected, the servo can be instructed to turn the white shaft back and forth.

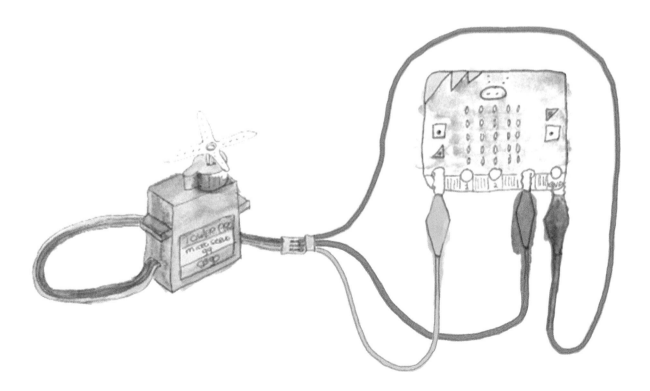

Programming

This project's programming is quite simple. The servo turns back and forth to make it look like the turkey's head is moving. Connecting a new piece of hardware, the servo, is the tricky part since they are not all the same.

These 180-degree servo motors move like a windshield wiper or a garage door opener. They rotate back and forth from 0 to 180 degrees. Your program can turn the motor by a precise amount. This makes servos reliable and more accurate than the type of DC motors found in toy cars or fans.

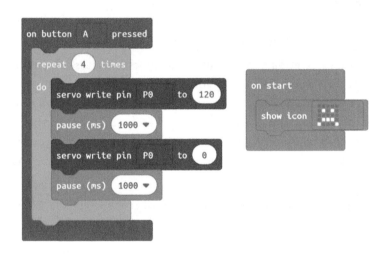

The `servo write pin` block is found under **Pins** in the **Advanced** Toolbox.

- Create a new project and name it *Turkey*
- Copy the program
- Read the program
- Predict what it does
- Test your program in the Simulator
- Connect the micro:bit to the computer and to the servo
- Download the new code to the micro:bit
- Test the new program on the micro:bit

Understanding the code

Most of this program should already be familiar to you. The new addition is the `servo write pin` block.

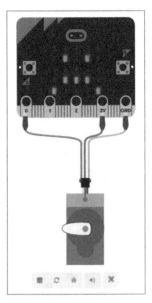

The `servo write pin` block takes two inputs, the pin where the servo is connected and the position (angle) it should turn to. The range of numbers for most servos, except for continuous ones, is 0 – 180.

Think of this like a windshield wiper. You tell the motor to turn to a specific location and then back again to create the wiping motion.

If you do not switch between different servo values, the motor will not turn. If I tell you to "Go Home!" then tell you, "Go Home!" again, you don't move, because you're still home.

Switching between two servo positions with a pause in between each movement is similar to the way in which you create a steady animation on the micro:bit display. If the pause is missing, or too short, the servo will not have time to move from one position to the next. You may feel it pulsing as it tries to move because the computer program runs a lot faster than the servo can move.

The Simulator will show you an image of how the servo should be connected. Your servo wires may be different colors.

Tips

- The 180 degree servo motor rotates from 0 to 180 degrees and then stops until told to move again. Another name for a 180-degree servo motor is a positional servo.
- Your battery must be full, otherwise the servo motor will not work.
- It is important to securely glue or tape the servo motor to the back of the big cardboard circle. This will prevent the servo motor from spinning.

Challenges

- Make the head move faster or slower.
- Can you add music to your turkey puppet? Remember, if you are adding a speaker, it must be connected to P0 and GND. You will need to move your servo connector to P1 or P2 and change your code.
- Program the buttons to turn the head in different directions.
- What other sorts of cardboard animations can you design?

Fruit Piano

Believe it or not, the micro:bit can be used to make a piano out of fruit. Touch a piece of fruit and a musical note or melody plays. Most fruit can conduct small amounts of electricity, in other words, fruit is conductive. Anything that is conductive can be part of a music playing circuit—all powered by your micro:bit. You may also experiment with other materials to see if they too are conductive.

Materials

micro:bit, USB cable & battery pack, 5 alligator clips, 1 piezo speaker (or headphones or earphones), 1 coin, and an assortment of materials like fruit, gummy candy, a cucumber, peppers, nails, and aluminum foil. You will not need the speaker if you have a micro:bit V2.

Make

1. Assemble your materials

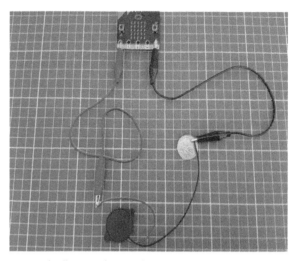

2. Attach alligator clips to the piezo speaker and use a coin to attach it to the GND pin.

3. Attach 2 other alligator clips to the P1 and P2 pins on the micro:bit. Connect the other side of these clips in the fruit, candy, or other materials you want to try.

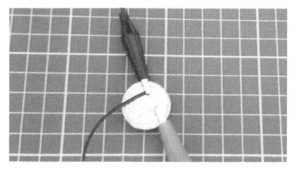

4. Attach 1 more alligator clip to the coin. This clip will be the ground connection that you use to touch the fruit and make the music.

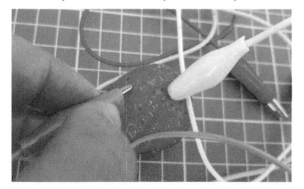

5. Once you program the micro:bit you can try out your piano. Touch the ground alligator clip to your fruit. Does your strawberry make music?

6. How about a cucumber or lemon? How about a glass of water?

Connections

Connect two alligator clips from the P1 and P2 pins to two pieces of fruit (or other conductive material).

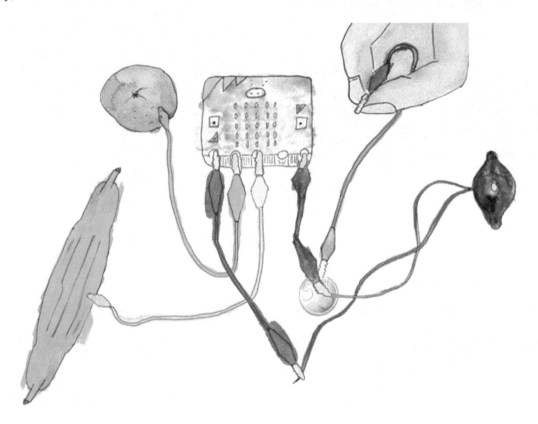

The piezo speaker or earphones must be connected to pin P0 and a coin that is connected to the GND on the micro:bit. The coin is used in this circuit to add space for multiple connections to GND. Another alligator clip is connected to this coin to create a grounded clip.

Touch this grounded alligator clip directly to the fruit to complete the circuit. You can also hold the metal part of this alligator clip in one hand and touch the fruit with your other hand... or nose...or elbow. Human beings are conductive too!

Sound is always output through pin P0 on the micro:bit and like any other circuit, must be grounded too. **If you have a micro:bit V2 (which has a built-in speaker) you can use P0 to add more fruit!**

Programming

The code for the fruit piano is really simple. When a circuit is closed by connecting a micro:bit pin (P1 or P2), a conductive piece of fruit, and ground, the micro:bit pin will trigger an event. Combine the fruit with the micro:bit's buttons and accelerometer and you're ready to jam!

Here are some blocks to try.

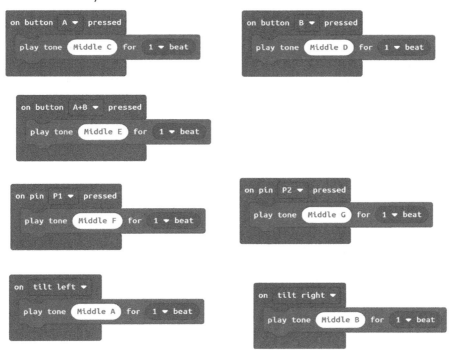

- Create a new project and name it *Fruit Piano*
- Copy the program
- Read the program
- Predict what it does
- Test your program on the Simulator
- Connect the micro:bit to your computer and a couple pieces of fruit
- Download the code to the micro:bit
- Test the program on the micro:bit

Understanding the code

`on pin` is the only new block introduced in this project. Its job is to do something if the circuit connected to that pin is closed, like when a piece of wired-up fruit is touched.

You should be familiar with the rest of the code. Choose different musical tones if you wish.

Tips

- Make sure that your speaker or pair of earphones is connected to P0 and GND (with a coin).
- The fruit must not touch each other.
- Make sure you connect an alligator clip to each piece of fruit. You may need to push it into the fruit to get a good connection.

Challenges

- Instead of playing a single tone, make each piece of fruit play a piece of a melody. Then play a song with those melodic fragments.
- Is water in a cup conductive?
- Can you replace a piece of fruit with a friend so that when you touch them, music is played?
- What else can you find that is conductive? Find new things to add to your fruit piano.

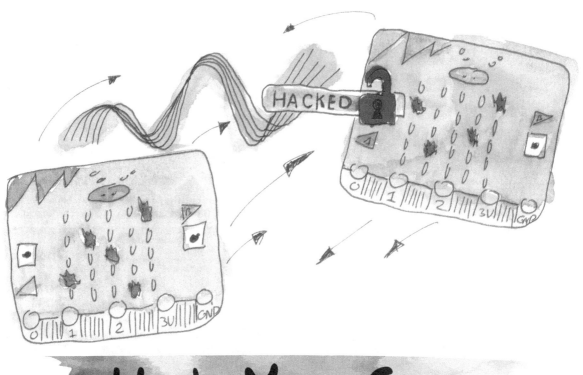

Hack Your Game

This project introduces the super cool radio features built into the micro:bit. You will learn how to send and receive messages between two micro:bits. Then we are going to improve upon the game you made in the *Your First Game* project by sending messages between two micro:bits for some two-player action.

In this version of the game, you will use the Radio function of the micro:bit to light up the onboard LED pixels on a different micro:bit. If you press A, one LED will light up on your micro:bit. When you press B, you will turn off one LED on your friend's micro:bit. With a bit of imagination, this will look like your character is eating your friend's electronic dots.

Materials
2 micro:bits, 1 USB cable & 2 battery packs, cardboard, scissors, *Hack Your Game* template, Velcro or tape.

Template
Use the *Hack Your Game* template for the game controllers or make your own. Find this downloadable template file at microbit.inventtolearn.com.

Make

1. Gather your materials.

2. Print and cut out the template and two square pieces of cardboard. Glue the template onto the cardboard.

3. Make a hole in the cardboard and attach the battery on the back side of the game controllers.

4. Attach the battery to the back of the cardboard with tape.

5. Attach your micro:bit with Velcro or tape.

6. Your game is ready to program and play.

Tips

- Use tape or Velcro to attach the micro:bit and the battery pack to the cardboard game controller. Do not glue them.

LED war

Now, make a game you can play between two micro:bits. This is similar to the simple game you made in the project *Your First Game*.

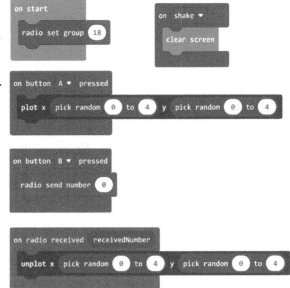

When you press A, an LED will light on your micro:bit. By pressing B, you will turn off an LED on the other micro:bit. If all your LEDs are on, you win the game!

Programming - LED war

Create the following program in MakeCode.

- Name the file *LED War* and save it
- Test the code in the MakeCode Simulator
- Download the program to both micro:bits. Do this by connecting one micro:bit at a time and downloading the code to each micro:bit
- Play the game and debug if necessary

Understanding the code - LED war

`on start` sets the channel for radio communication.

`on shake` clears the display on your micro:bit.

When button A is pressed, an LED is lit at a random position on your micro:bit. If that pixel is already lit, it stays that way. Your opponent is trying to light their LEDs and unlight yours.

The `plot x y` block turns on one of the pixels in the micro:bit display.

The x and y values are randomly picked from a number between 0 and 4 using the `pick random` block.

When you press button B, a number is broadcast via radio.

When your micro:bit or your opponent's micro:bit "hears" any number in the `on radio received` block, a random pixel is turned off.

The `unplot x y` block turns off one of the pixels in the micro:bit display.

Tip

- If you are working in a place with a lot of walls or other interference, you can increase your radio signal strength by setting the `radio set transmit power` to 7 (in the **Radio...more** Toolbox).

Challenges

- Can you turn on 2 LEDs at the same time?
- Can you also turn off 2 or more LEDs simultaneously?
- Can you add a sound when you light one of your pixels or zap one of your opponents?
- Can you add a timer to your game to make it more exciting to play?

Radio Communication

micro:bits can send messages to a seemingly unlimited number of other micro:bits, as long as they are tuned to the same channel. That is why it is important that you specify the channel used for communication. Otherwise, other micro:bits can listen in or spy on your communication.

One of the coolest features of the micro:bit is its ability to send and receive messages wirelessly between multiple micro:bits. This superpower may be used to create a remote controlled vehicle, multiplayer game, receive data from another site, or even to create simulations of insect colonies. Radio communication on the micro:bit allows for an infinite number of inventions, especially if you understand how it works. This collection of activities demonstrates ways in which MakeCode's radio blocks may be used to supercharge future projects. Master these tools and all sorts of possibilities will be revealed!

Think of it this way—a radio station has a tower high atop a city and it broadcasts an endless stream of information. If your radio is not turned on or tuned to that channel, the invisible information flies right past you and is "caught" by radios that are within range, turned on, and tuned to that specific channel or station. micro:bit broadcasting works the same way. If "someone" is listening, it does something with the information received, otherwise that info just evaporates.

Any micro:bits powered on, within 70 meters of the sender, and programmed to listen for data broadcast on that channel might receive that information.

Programming - Radio test

First, create a simple program using the radio function of the micro:bit. It is important to set the channel of your radio group to be the same as the channel your friend's micro:bit is tuned to. There are 256 different radio channels to choose from, numbered from 0 to 255. Your micro:bits should be within about 50 meters of each other to use the radio function. This might be less if there are walls or lots of other computers around.

Important! This project requires that the same program be downloaded to each of your two micro:bits! When you are working with more than one micro:bit, you must pair each of them individually to MakeCode.

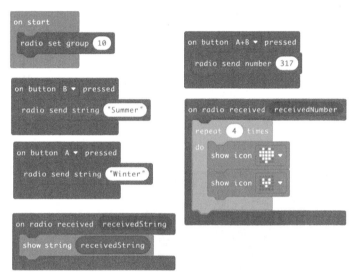

- Create a new project and name it *Radio Test*
- Copy the program
- Connect the first micro:bit to your computer and pair it
- Download the code to the micro:bit
- Connect the second micro:bit to your computer. You must pair this micro:bit as well.
- Download the code to the second micro:bit
- Be sure that both micro:bits are programmed and powered on!
- Test the new program on each micro:bit

To put the `receivedString` variable in the `show string` block, click and drag the `receivedString` oval from the top of the `on radio received` `receivedString` container into the hole in the `show string` block.

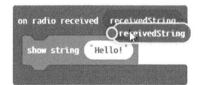

Understanding the code - Radio test

The `on start` block sets the radio channel for the micro:bits to be sure both micro:bits are set to the same channel. If lots of people nearby choose the same channel, there may be interference. Therefore, pick a unique channel for your two micro:bits to use.

When the A button is pressed, broadcast the string, "Winter."

When button B is pressed, broadcast the string, "Summer."

`on radio received` `receivedString` "hears" a string being broadcast. It grabs it from the air and shows that string on the micro:bit display.

When buttons A and B are pressed together, a number is broadcast. The particular number does not matter here since this program only checks to see if *some* number is broadcast.

When a number is broadcast, the other micro:bit will be triggered to run the instructions in the `on radio received` `receivedNumber` block. In this case, a short simple animation will be displayed.

Using radio in the MakeCode Simulator

If you use the radio function in your code, the MakeCode Simulator will show both the sending and receiving micro:bits. Click the A or B buttons onscreen in the Simulator to test your code.

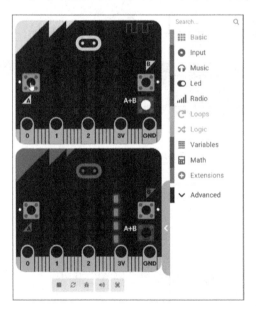

Challenges
- Can you slow down the animation?
- Can you download the code to more than two micro:bits and have a message passing party?
- Change the messages you send.

What's the difference?

Can you compare this new version (below) with the previous code? How will it change the behavior of your micro:bit?

If you cannot predict the way the result of the program changes, change the program to the new version and download it to your two micro:bits.

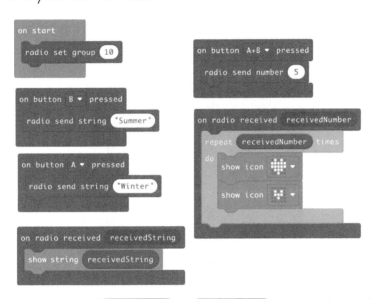

In on radio received , the input variable (receivedString or receivedNumber) can be dragged into another block as a replacement value.

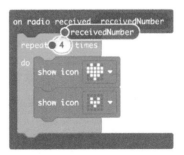

Change the numerical value in the on button A+B pressed block and see what happens.

Understanding the code - What's the difference?

The first version of this code just uses a number as a signal to any micro:bits listening for a number to be broadcast.

The second version of this code sends a number, and that value is used to tell the repeat block how many times to loop the animation.

Random radio

Now that you have the micro:bits communicating, write a new program so that when you shake your micro:bit, one of two words will appear randomly on the other micro:bit. Use the same code, just add an `on shake` block to replace the button controls.

In this simple example, the block `pick random true or false` picks true or false randomly. If true, the block in the "if" slot runs. If the random pick is false, the block in the "else" slot runs. Every time you shake the micro:bit, a random message is sent.

This is like flipping a coin.

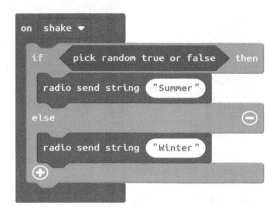

Challenge

- Can you send a number from one micro:bit to another and have a different animation play depending on the number sent as the message?
- Try the project *Hack Your Game* with more micro:bits.

Distance Detector

The micro:bit can communicate with others by sending and receiving radio signals. This project uses two micro:bits to detect when they get close to each other. When the micro:bits are near each other, an alert will sound, warning that you are too close.

You and a friend can wear these distance alarms, put one on your little brother, or maybe even on two pets.

Materials
2 micro:bits, 2 USB cable & battery packs, 4 alligator clips, 2 piezo speakers, cardboard, scissors, glue, tape, tape measure, Distance Detector template.

Note: if you are using a micro:bit V2 you do not need to connect speakers.

Make

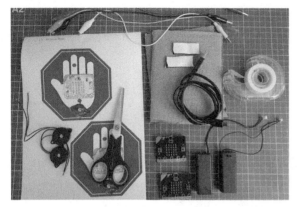

1. Assemble your materials.

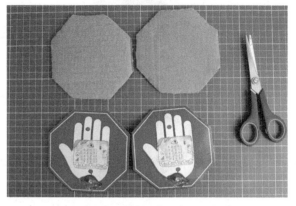

2. Cut two rounds of cardboard and cut out the template of the distance detector (or you can make your own template and color it).

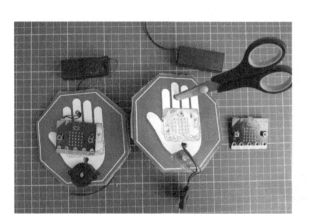

3. Glue the template on the cardboard. On each template, make a hole for the wires to come through connecting the piezo speaker and battery pack to the micro:bit.

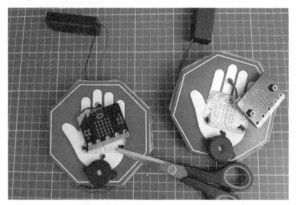

4. Punch two holes for the alligator clips on each template. One clip connects to P0 and the other to GND on the micro:bit.

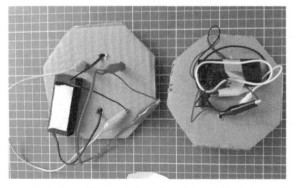

5. Attach the cables and tape the cables and battery pack behind your detectors.

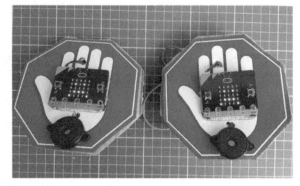

6. Your two distance detectors are now ready for coding and testing.

Connections

The piezo (speaker) must be connected to pin P0 and GND of the micro:bit. Make sure that the metal parts of the alligator clips don't touch each other when they are taped to the back of your distance detector. If you have a micro:bit V2, you do not need to attach a speaker.

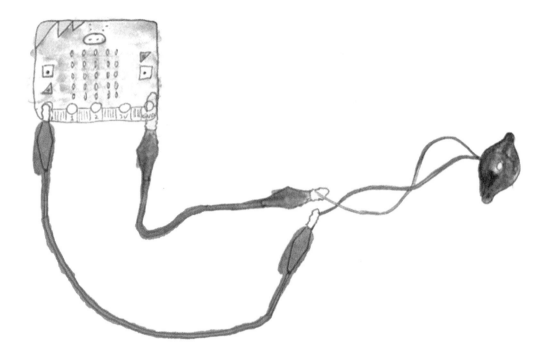

Template

Use the *Distance Detector* template or make your own. Find this downloadable template file at microbit.inventtolearn.com.

Programming

Each micro:bit uses the radio function to check the signal strength of the other micro:bit. A higher number indicates a strong signal and is a clue that the micro:bits are close to each other. To figure out how close they are, you will create a program to test the signal strength. When working with sensors it is quite common to write a program to check the normal range of values being reported and use those results in the invention. In this case, we need to test how signal strength is related to the distance between the two micro:bits. The same program needs to be downloaded onto both micro:bits in order to run this test. If you haven't already paired the second micro:bit to MakeCode, you must do this before you download.

- Start a new project and name it *Distance Detector*
- Create the program
- Read the program and predict what it does
- Connect the micro:bit to your computer
- Download the new code to the micro:bit
- Connect the second micro:bit and download the same code to it

Tip

- The `radio set transmit power` block is in the **... more** menu in the **Radio** section of the Toolbox.

Testing the Distance Detector

- Make sure both micro:bits are powered on and near each other
- Press the A button on one of the micro:bits and see the value displayed.
- Move the two micro:bits a little further apart. Press the A button to observe how the signal strength changes. Keep track of the distance and the signal strength.
- Try moving one micro:bit 1.5 meters (approximately 5 feet) from the second running micro:bit, press the A button, and make note of the signal strength value for that distance. Test this a few times to make sure you get a relatively consistent value. We will use 1.5 meters to program our Distance Detector.

Understanding the code

When the program starts, a heart lights up on the display.

Tell each micro:bit to set its radio channel to 1. You can choose any channel (1–255) to avoid interference with other nearby micro:bits as long as your two micro:bits are set to the same channel.

Next, we tell the micro:bit radio to operate at its most powerful signal strength. 6 is the default, 7 is the maximum broadcast power.

The `forever` block is constantly broadcasting the number 0. It doesn't really matter what it is yelling unless another micro:bit is listening for that particular message. This is just like how a music or news radio station works. They broadcast and some number of radios are listening. If your radio is off, the signal is still being sent, even if you are not listening.

When you press the A button, the value being sent via radio will be displayed by the `show number` block. In this case, it shows the value of the signal strength.

In essence, you have built and programmed a tool to measure signal strength, and are using it to represent distance.

Programming - Automatic distance detector

Add the following code so that micro:bits respond automatically if they are closer than 1.5 meters apart. When you are too close, the micro:bit will be sad. Otherwise, it will be happy.

The number you wrote down when your micro:bits were 1.5 meters apart will be entered in the **if** line of the `if then else block` of this program. The example below uses –60. Replace that number with the value you recorded.

Sensor values may change or fluctuate under real world conditions. Whenever you use a sensor to produce a particular action, it is worth running a test to see if the values used in your program are still accurate. Values like signal strength may need to be calibrated if you use different micro:bits, move to a different location, or have objects or walls in between the micro:bits.

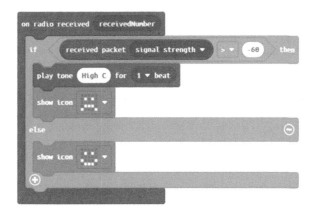

- Download the new program (along with the original blocks) to both micro:bits.

A tricky bit of code

This last bit of code requires some new skills to build the blocks.

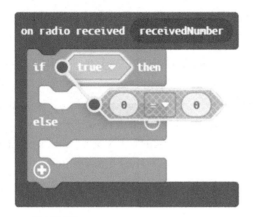

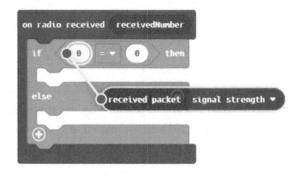

1. Drag the `if then else` block from Logic Toolbox into the `radio received` block.

Drag the `0 = 0` block from the Logic Toolbox to replace the `true` block that's already in the `if then else` block.

2. If/then commands are called conditionals. They do something when a condition is true. The `if 0 = 0 then` block includes a drop-down menu that lets you select equality or inequality symbols. Then you can replace the zeros and compare one value with another.

Drag a `received packet` block from the Radio Toolbox to replace the first 0.

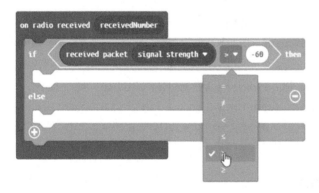

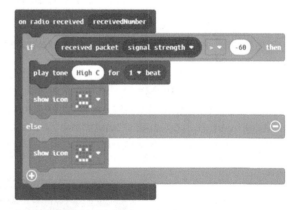

3. Change = into > by clicking on the small arrow.

Change the 0 to -60.

In this case, we are building an instruction to check if the signal strength is greater than -60.

4. Drag `play tone` from the Music Toolbox and pick a tone.

Drag `show icon` from the Basic Toolbox and add to the `if` section of the `if then else` block.

Drag another show icon to the `else` section of the `if then else` block.

Understanding the code - Automatic distance detector

The `on radio received` `receivedNumber` block waits until a radio message that is a number is broadcast. When that happens, the rest of the instructions are run. Since `forever` is continuously broadcasting the number 0, this set of instructions will run over and over again—testing the signal strength.

The range of signal strength is from –128 (weak) to –42 (strong). This can be a bit confusing because the range uses negative numbers. Therefore, testing that the micro:bit is *closer* uses *greater than* in the if conditional block. Would –50 mean that the micro:bits are closer or farther apart than if the signal strength is –80?

Challenge

- Using two micro:bits, design your own smart shield, wristband, hat, or burglar alarm.

Saving & Sharing Your Code

Now that you have created a few micro:bit projects, it is a good idea to learn how to save, open, and share files with others.

Save a project

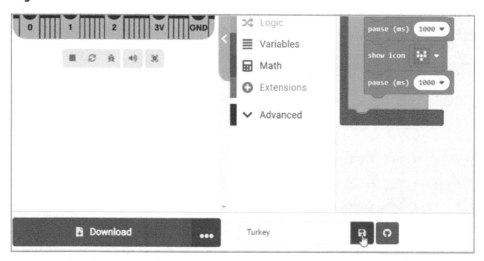

- To the right of the **Download** button is a field where you see the name of your project
- To save the project with that name, click the disk icon next to the name field
- Your project will be saved in the download folder of your computer

When you work on a complex project, it is a good idea to save multiple versions of your project anytime you make a significant change. Name and save your project versions with names like project1, project2, project3... or game1, game2, game3... This way, if you need to go back a version, you have that file and can simply open it and continue from there.

Open saved projects

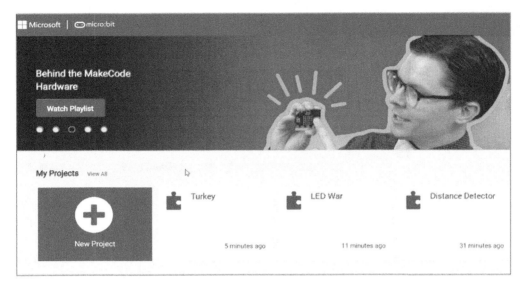

- If you saved projects, you will find them by pressing the **Home** icon on the MakeCode website. Go to makecode.microbit.org or click on **Home**.
- Click on a listed project to open that project and edit it in MakeCode.
- If you change the code, save it under a new name or it will overwrite your saved program.

Tips

- When you save your project, use a name that reminds you of your project
- Save the file with a new name when you change your project or add new features

Caution!

If you delete the cookies in your web browser, or change to a different browser, your files in the Home area of the MakeCode website will be lost. This is a good reason to save your files to your hard drive.

Open projects from your computer

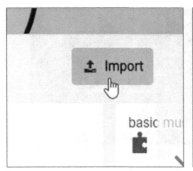 

- If you saved your projects locally (to a hard drive or USB stick), you may open those projects in MakeCode. Go to makecode.microbit.org or click on **Home**.
- Click on **Import** (on the right above any saved projects).
- There you have 3 options: Import from your local hard drive, from a (GitHub) URL, or from your GitHub Repo. In most cases, you will import from a local hard drive. Select the file from your Download folder (unless you saved elsewhere) and click **Go ahead**!
- You can also drag a project file into your MakeCode Workspace and it will open there.

Share your project in the cloud

To share your project, click on the **Share** icon at the top right of the MakeCode screen

- In the dialog box, you can change the project name, and click **Publish project**
- In the next screen, a long URL (website link) is created for you
- Copy the URL and use it in your documents, websites, blogs, email, or other places
- You also have the ability to share your project via FaceBook, Twitter, or in the MakeCode forum
- To embed your project in another web page or blog post, click the **Embed** dropdown link to copy HTML that will display your code, a live mini-editor, or the micro:bit Simulator. This allows you to create tutorials online to explain your project to others.

Open projects with a link

If you shared your project to the cloud, you can reopen the project using the link. For example, click on this link: makecode.microbit.org/_5VzFgibJUam2 A new webpage will open, and you will see your code and the name of the project. Click the edit button to use or change the project.

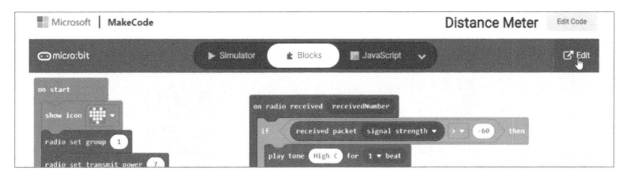

Challenges

- Open a MakeCode project from your download folder
- Email a project to a friend
- Embed a project in a web page or blog post
- Drag a .hex file in your download folder directly into the MakeCode editor to open a project

It's Alive!

The Bionic Doll

Let's hack a doll by replacing its eyes with LEDs. You may find other creatures around the house to animate too. They can be cool, kooky, or spooky. Be sure not to operate on a toy anyone in your family cares about!

Materials

micro:bit, USB cable and battery pack, 2 alligator clips, 2 LEDs (5mm or 10mm), utility knife, scissors, marker, doll you have permission to alter.

Make

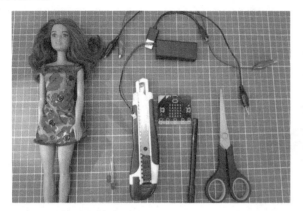

1. Gather the materials you need.

2. Remove the doll's head.

3. Use the utility knife to carefully cut a hole in the back of the doll head. This should give you access to the LED legs. Be careful and ask for help if you are not accustomed to using a utility knife. Trim the doll's hair with scissors near the hole if necessary.

4. Poke holes in the eyes of the doll large enough to hold the LEDs, but not too big.

5. Push the LEDs into the doll's eyes.

6. Position the two LEDs so that the two positive legs can be twisted together. Then twist the two negative legs together. Make sure that the positive legs do not touch negative legs and short the circuit.

7. Connect a red alligator clip to the positive LED legs and a black alligator clip to the two negative LED legs. (Your alligator clips might be different colors.)

8. Program the micro:bit and test your code and connections. Make sure that the eyes light up before reattaching the doll's head to its body.

9. Carefully attach the head back on the doll and check again to ensure that the lights are still working.

Connections

Connect the alligator clip joining the positive (long) legs of the LEDs to either P0, P1, or P2 on the micro:bit. The negative (short) legs of the LEDs must always be connected to GND. In this program, the LEDs are connected to P0.

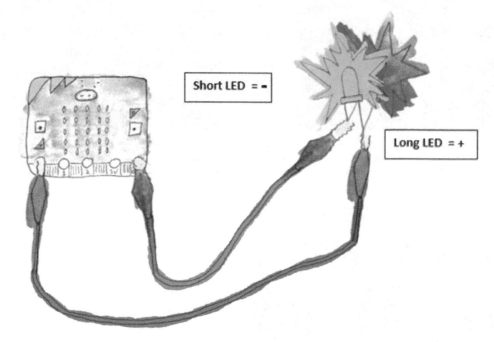

Short LED = –

Long LED = +

Tips

- Most LEDs have a long (positive +) leg and short (negative –) leg.
- To help you remember which wire is which, use red alligator clips for power and black for ground (GND). This is standard in electrical connections.
- Before you attach the head of the doll to its body, test the LEDs. You can do this with the micro:bit—see the project *Hack Your Game* for details.
- If it is difficult to reach the LEDs, create a bigger hole in the back of the doll's head.
- If you move the clip to a different pin on the micro:bit, don't forget to change the code to match.

Programming

- Create a new project and name it *Doll*
- Copy the program.
- The Simulator will show the signal being sent to P0. When a 1 is sent, the pin turns on. When a 0 is sent, the pin turns off.
- Connect the micro:bit to your computer
- Download the new code to the micro:bit

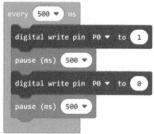

Understanding the code

The `every` block loops forever, like the `forever` block. The every block is found in the **Loops** section of the Toolbox. It works like an `on start` block in that it runs automatically. The instructions inside the `every` block run at the interval you specify, in this case, 500 ms.

This code will run and the lights will blink forever, or until you unplug the micro:bit from power.

Challenges

- Change the number of times the eyes flash or the speed at which they flash.
- Program a button to trigger some new action.
- Make each eye blink independently.
- Program some eye animation sequence.
- Use a second micro:bit as a remote control for your doll/creature.

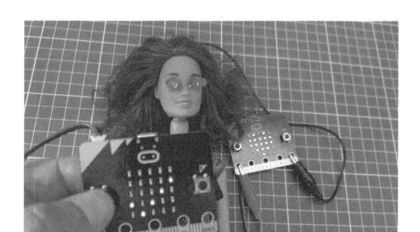

Monster Box

Let's turn a box into a monster with a head that responds when you shine light on it. All sorts of boxes, cartons, art supplies, and repurposed junk may be used to make an original monster. Since servo motors require more power than the micro:bit battery pack has on its own, we will use a USB power bank, the kind of portable charger used with cellphones.

Materials

micro:bit, USB cable, USB power bank, 3 alligator clips (preferably ones with male pins on one end), 180-degree servo motor, 3 ping pong balls, construction paper, box, googly eyes, string or fishing line, flashlight or cell phone light, hot glue gun, scissors, tape, glue sticks.

Make

1. Collect all of the material you need.

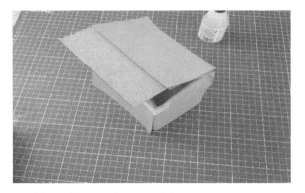

2. Fold your box so it has a top lid.

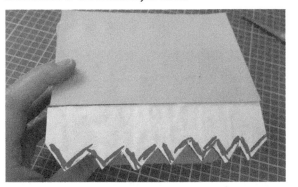

3. Make some teeth for your monster.

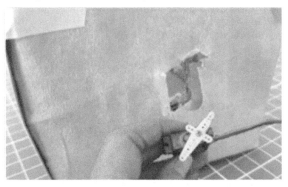

3. Cut a hole in the side of the box just large enough to fit the servo motor you are using.

4. Glue or tape the servo motor firmly in the hole.

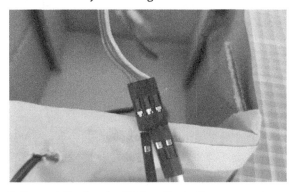

5. Connect the 3 male alligator clips to the servo motor.

6. Make holes in the box for the cable of the power bank and the alligator clips for the micro:bit. The alligator clips need to connect to GND, 3V and P1. Check the Connections diagram on the next page.

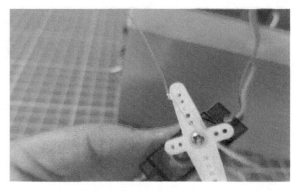

7. Connect a plastic string to the servo motor.

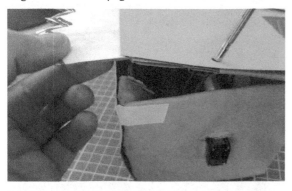

8. Make a small hole in the lid of the box, just above the servo motor.

9. Make sure your servo motor is 'down' before you adjust your string to the lid of the box.

10. Close the box with the string really tight. Test your code and the servo. Adjust if necessary.

11. Decorate your monster even more and have fun.

Connections

Connect the positional servo motor to the P1, 3V, and GND pins on the micro:bit.

Connect the dark (usually black or brown) cable on your servo to GND, the red servo cable to 3V, and the remaining wire (usually yellow or orange) on your servo to P0. There is a more complete explanation of how the servo works in the *Turkey Trot* project.

If you use alligator clips with the clip on one end and a male lead (pin) on the other, these will fit nicely into your servo connection cable. If you are using regular alligator clips, you may insert a piece of wire into one end of each alligator clip. That wire plugs into the female connector on the servo.

Using P1 or P2 as connection pins for the servo leaves P0 open if you want to add sound to your monster by connecting a speaker or headphones.

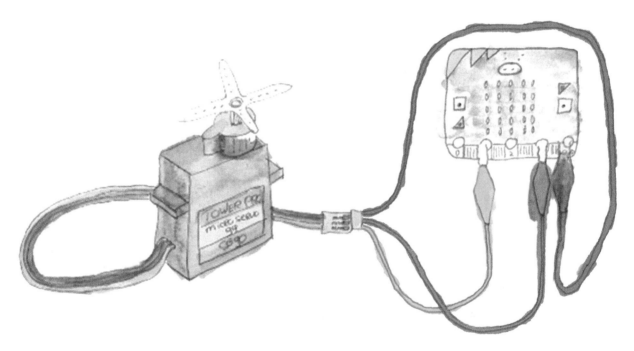

Tips

- Make sure that the power bank is charged before putting it in the box.
- Adjust the servo motor to tighten the string connected to the box lid.
- Use a flashlight or the light on a cellphone to wake the monster.

Programming

In this project, you will use the light sensor of the micro:bit to bring the monster to life. New blocks will be introduced for reading a light sensor, controlling a servo, and displaying a bar graph of sensor data.

The servo motor will turn when the micro:bit detects a change in the light levels received by the sensor. This creates the illusion of the monster's mouth chomping.

We used a positional servo motor in the *Turkey Trot* project. This time we will use a different block to control the servo.

The designers of MakeCode anticipated that people might create new things to attach to the micro:bit. Programming those things sometimes requires new blocks. So, clicking on **Extensions** in the Toolbox allows you to search for the functionality you wish to add, and loads new blocks into the MakeCode software.

In the *Turkey Trot* project, we controlled the servo motor with a `digital write` block. That block sends a number to a pin and doesn't care what is connected to that pin. If we know we will be using servo motors, adding the servo extensions and using the `set servo` block makes our code more precise and easier to read. In this case the servo behaves exactly the same way as it did with the `digital write` block. We just did not want to confuse you with adding extensions to MakeCode earlier in the book.

There are two types of servo motors, some that rotate 180 degrees (like a windshield wiper) and others that spin all the way around with a rotational motion of 360 degrees. In this project, we use a positional servo that turns from 0 to 180 degrees.

Create the following blocks in MakeCode:

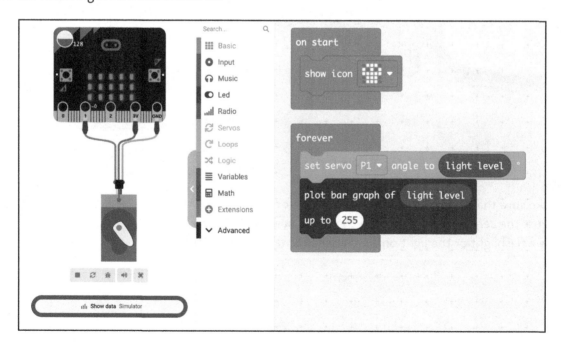

The Invent to Learn Guide to the micro:bit

- Place a `show icon` block in the `on start` block and pick a shape to display
- Go to **Extensions** in the Toolbox, then click on **Servo**. There will now be new servo blocks in the Toolbox. These will save with your project.
- Drag the `set servo` block from **Servos** in the Toolbox into the `forever` block
- Drag the light level reporter block from **Input** in the Toolbox into the oval input where the number 90 currently appears in the `set servo` block.
- Add the `plot bar graph` block from the **Led** panel under the `set servo` block in `forever`.
- Either copy the `light level` block or drag out as new one from the **Input** panel and place it in the first line of the `plot bar graph` block in `forever`. Change the "up to" value to 255.
- Name and save the project, *Monster*.
- Test your code in the MakeCode Simulator. Using the special servo blocks adds a servo to the Simulator. Change the light level by clicking and dragging the virtual light meter in the top left-hand corner of the Simulator. The simulated servo should respond to the virtual light meter.
- Download the code to the micro:bit.

Understanding the code

The program starts by showing an icon on the micro:bit display. This is a good way to indicate that your program is downloaded and running.

The `forever` block continuously sets the angle of the servo to the current value being detected by the light sensor. The light sensor reading will be zero in the dark, up to 255 as light levels increase.

`plot bar graph` creates an image on the 5x5 grid of LEDs that grows and shrinks depending on the input. Changing the "up to" field to 255 tells MakeCode that is the maximum value to plot.

You are replacing a fixed number for the servo setting with a number that will change as the light sensor reports different values. So, the servo will turn as the light gets brighter and dimmer.

The light sensor reports values from 0–255, but the servo only turns 0–180 degrees. This means any value greater than 180 is ignored and the servo stays at the angle of 180 until a lesser value is read by the sensor.

Precision programming

If you were building a more precise machine and wanted the light sensor to more accurately control the position of the 180-degree servo, you could change the code to look like this.

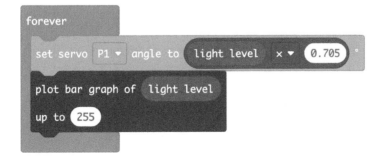

Can you explain why we multiply the light level by 0.705 to control the servo? This isn't a perfect example since the servo only turns by positive integers, but there are times when you might need such accuracy while programming.

Extremely precise programming

There is an even more accurate and efficient way to use the light sensor values to control the position of the 180-degree servo. Modify the code like this.

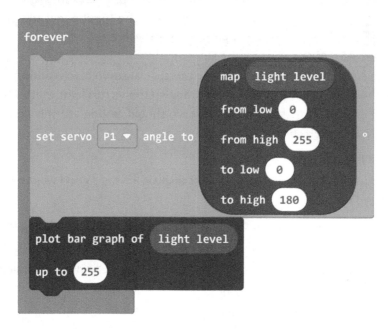

The map block is found in the **Pins** panel in the **Advanced** Toolkit. This block precisely converts one range of numbers onto another range. In this case, it takes the light sensor value (a number between 0 and 255) and calculates the corresponding value from 0 to 180 to use as the servo position. This is a more precise way to control the servo and good programming practice.

Mapping is often useful when using sensors, since different sensors report different ranges of values. This block is only used for pin input values, but there is an equally useful map block in the **Math** panel for all other mathematical range conversions.

Challenges

- Add sound to your monster.
- Can you also use the temperature sensor to control your monster? Wake it up with a hair dryer perhaps?
- Use another micro:bit as a remote control for your monster.
- If you have a micro:bit V2, can loud sounds trigger your monster?

Fortune Teller

Program a micro:bit fortune teller machine. Ask a question, shake your machine, and predict the future!

Materials

micro:bit, 1 USB cable & battery pack, colorful paper, small cardboard box, glue, tape. Use the Fortune Teller template or decorate the box any way you wish.

Make

1. Assemble your materials.

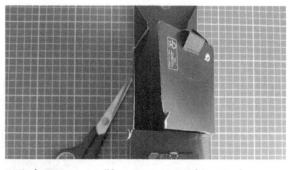

2. Find a square small box approximately 4-6 inches or make one out of cardboard.

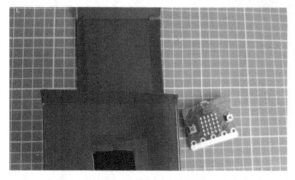

3. Cut a hole in the front of the box, so the LED display of the micro:bit is visible.

4. Cut out stars from colored paper or felt.

5. Tape the battery and micro:bit securely inside the box. Place the micro:bit so the LEDs show through the hole in the box.

6. Decorate your fortune telling machine with stars or other magical symbols.

Template

Download the template for *Fortune Teller* or make your own. Find this downloadable template file at microbit.inventtolearn.com.

Programming

Let's see how a physical gesture can be used to create a random result.

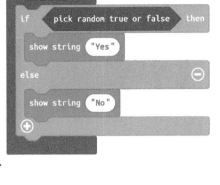

- Create a new project and name it *Fortune Teller*
- Copy the program
- Read the program and predict what it does
- Test your program on the Simulator by clicking the **Shake** button
- Connect the micro:bit to your computer
- Download the new code to the micro:bit
- Shake the Fortune Teller as you ask a simple yes or no question.

Understanding the code

When the micro:bit is shaken, the `if/then` block checks **IF** a conditional statement is true or false and **THEN** does something if the result is true.

The block `pick random true or false` randomly reports "true" or "false."

Clicking the + button on the `if/then` block allows you to add a consequence that will occur if the statement tested is false (**ELSE**).

When shaken, the micro:bit will display the word "Yes" or "No" at random.

Tips

- If you click on the **+** more if/else options will appear. If you press on the **−** the options will be deleted. Try this out.
- Mouse over a block for a second or two and an explanation of the block will pop up.

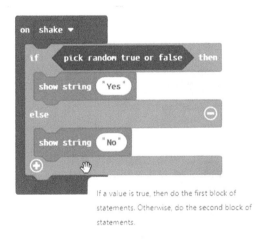

If a value is true, then do the first block of statements. Otherwise, do the second block of statements.

Create a smarter program with variables

Start by creating a new variable, called **fortune**. Open **Variables** in the Toolbox and click on **Make a Variable**. After you name the variable, it will appear in the **Variable** panel.

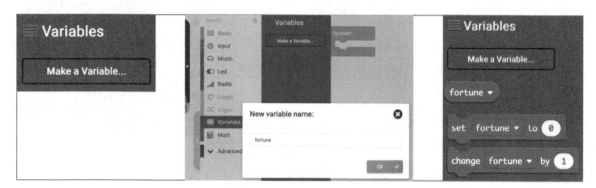

When you create a variable, MakeCode automatically makes two additional blocks that might be useful. One sets the current value of the variable to 0. The other adds 1 to the variable. Of course, you can change the 0 and 1 to other values if you want.

The variable, **fortune**, will be used to store a random number. The random number will be used to tell the Fortune Teller which fortune to display.

Create the following program.

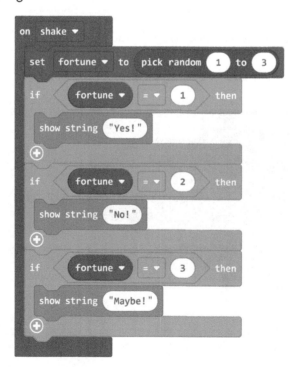

Understanding the code

When the micro:bit is shaken, set a variable, **fortune**, to a random number between 1 and 3.

The `if/then` block checks the value of the random number picked and displays "Yes," "No," or "Maybe" on the micro:bit based on the value.

Ask a question such as, "Will I get a pony for my birthday?" Then shake the Fortune Teller to reveal the answer!

Programming more dramatic fortune telling

Let's take a bit of time to make your Fortune Teller cooler. Now when shaken, the program will clear the display (in case anything is on it), dramatically pause for one second, tell your fortune, and then display an icon on the micro:bit indicating that it is ready to tell another fortune.

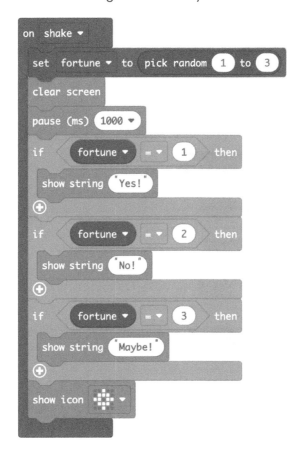

Faster fortunes

Since the `show string` block causes characters to scroll by on the micro:bit display, you may find the Fortune Teller behaves too slowly. Displaying an icon instead of text, as shown in the program here, may increase the speed of your Fortune Teller. You may want to delete the pause and clear screen blocks for even faster fortunes.

If you have a micro:bit version 2

The V2 micro:bit's microphone may be used as a sound sensor to trigger events. Revise your code so the program starts when a loud noise is detected. Add sound effects to make your Fortune Teller more mysterious.

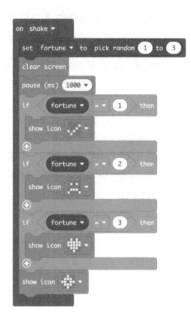

Challenges

- Add other fortunes to your code. (Meh, yup, nah, perhaps...)
- Replace the pause with a musical "beep boop" when the micro:bit is shaken.
- Transform your project from fortune teller to digital fortune cookie. How will the messages change? How many fortunes can you include?
- Can you use the radio functionality of the micro:bit to send a fortune to another micro:bit?

Space Game

In this project you will make a two-button controller to play a space game. Arcade-style buttons are connected to the micro:bit and special game blocks from within MakeCode are used to bring the game to life. This project is inspired by the classic arcade game, "Space Invaders."

Materials
micro:bit, USB cable & 1 battery pack, 5 alligator clips, 2 game buttons, cardboard, scissors, tape, 1 coin, Space Game template.

Make

1. Gather all necessary materials.

2. Use the template to cut out the cardboard game controller. Make two holes for the buttons.

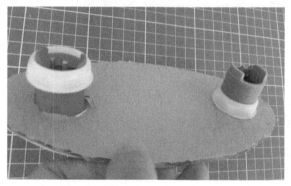

3. Push the buttons through the cardboard and turn the small rings to tighten the buttons on the game controller. If your buttons do not have such rings, use a bit of hot glue to hold the buttons in place.

4. Punch a hole for the battery cable, and three small holes for the alligator clips to connect to P0, P1, and GND while also holding the micro:bit in place.

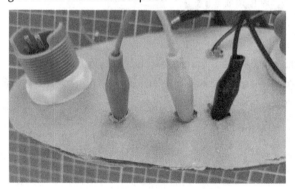

5. Push the tips of the alligator clips through the cardboard.

6. Attach them to P0, P1, and the GND pins on the micro:bit.

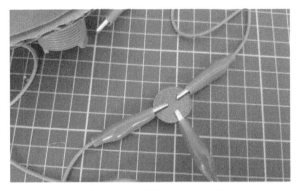

7. Use a coin to allow each of the ground cables to connect to GND on the micro:bit.

Connect the ground cable connected to GND on the micro:bit to a coin.

Next, attach the ground cable from each button to the coin as well.

You may wish to then tape all three alligator clips to the coin.

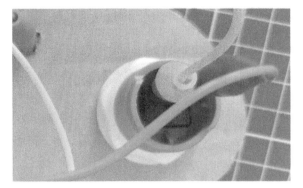

8. Each button should have two places to attach wires to, labeled + and -.

On one button, attach two alligator clips.

Attach the clip connected to the + side to pin P0.

Attach the clip connected to the - side to GND.

9. Repeat for the other button, connecting it to P1 and GND.

10. The wiring should end up looking like this.

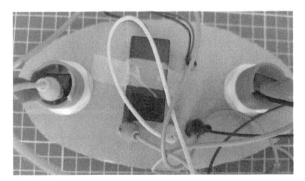

11. Attach a battery pack by taping it to the underside of the cardboard game controller.

12. Download the code and test your Space Game.

Connections

Two buttons are attached to P0 and P1. The ground connections from both buttons need to be connected to GND on the micro:bit. It is difficult to attach two alligator clips to one pin. To get around this, a coin may be used to join the two button ground cables to GND on the micro:bit. If you find that a button is not working, check the connections and make sure that the positive and ground cables are not reversed.

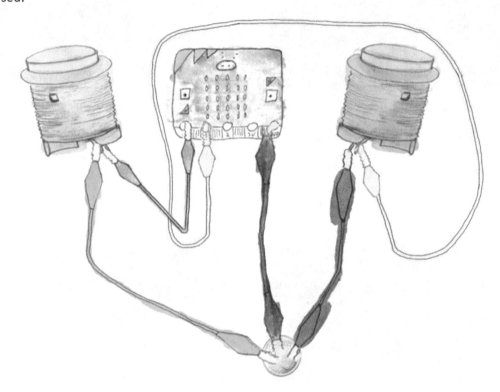

Template

Download the *Space Game* template for this project or make your own. Find this downloadable template file at microbit.inventtolearn.com.

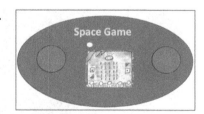

Programming - Move the spaceship

The code for the Space Game is more complicated than in previous projects. To help, you will use the preprogrammed game functions in MakeCode. Those blocks are found in the **Games** blocks in the **Advanced** Toolbox.

Let's build the code a bit at a time. First, program the micro:bit so your spaceship can move left to right. Then add an alien that slowly drops down on your ship. Finally, add the ability to zap your alien with a laser ray effect.

To make a moving spaceship, the first thing to do is create a variable called **ship**. The ship will be one of the characters in your game.

- Go to **Variables** in the Toolbox
- Click on **Make a Variable...**
- Name the variable, *ship*.
- Now that variable is ready to use in your code!
- Create the following blocks in MakeCode.

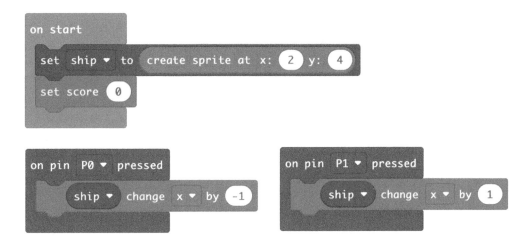

Understanding the code - Move the spaceship

When the program starts, your spaceship appears in the starting position and the score of the game is set to zero. Initializing variables is common in lots of computer programs, particularly games.

Speaking of variables, remember that there will be no variable named **ship** unless you create it.

The ship is a single pixel (LED) on the micro:bit display. Using the special Game block `create sprite` creates a variable that is more than just a number, it now represents a "sprite," a little LED creature that you can move around the micro:bit display. Sprites are easy to move, can be bright or dim, and can tell when they bump into things—all important for programming games.

At the start, your ship is created (lit) and placed at the bottom middle of the micro:bit LEDs (x=2 and y=4).

Each game starts with a score of zero.

If your arcade buttons are connected properly, you can move the ship to the left or right by pressing each button. The program responds by changing the X value of the variable **ship**.

If you don't have arcade buttons, it's easy to replace the `on pin` blocks with `on button` blocks and use the A and B buttons to move the ship.

Understanding the micro:bit's LED display

Although it's only five pixels by five pixels in size, the grid of LEDs on the micro:bit is a coordinate system. Each LED is assigned a position on the X and Y axis, so you can turn them on and off by using the correct X and Y values. However, you may find that this micro:bit coordinate system is different from what you are used to in math class.

The LEDs on the X axis are numbered from 0–4 from left to right.

The Y axis LEDs are also numbered from 0–4, but they run from top to bottom. In other words, the top left LED is (0 , 0) and the bottom right LED is (4 , 4).

If you mouse over a pixel in the Simulator, MakeCode reminds you of its coordinates.

Lots of different programming languages and devices use coordinates differently. As long as you know the rule, you can turn the LEDs on and off with ease.

Programming - Alien

Now that you can move your spaceship side to side, it's time to add an alien.

- Add the following stack of blocks to the spaceship code already in MakeCode, read it, and see if you can understand how it works
- Remember to make a new variable, **alien**
- As always, you may test the code in the MakeCode Simulator
- Download the new code to the micro:bit

```
forever
    set alien ▾ to  create sprite at  x:  pick random  0  to  4   y:  0
    pause (ms)  150 ▾
    repeat  4  times
    do
            alien ▾  change  y ▾  by  1
        pause (ms)  500 ▾
        if     is  alien ▾  touching  ship ▾     then
            game over
        ⊕
    if     is  alien ▾  touching  edge     then
        delete  alien ▾
    ⊕
```

Understanding the code - Alien

The `forever` block creates a new sprite, an alien attacking your ship. It first appears at a random position of x, and the y coordinate is equal to zero (the top row).

The alien falls down one row at a time with a small pause.

If the alien touches your ship, the game is over.

If the alien reaches the bottom of the display without hitting your ship, the alien is deleted.

Programming - Zap the alien

Once you have an alien, you can create an additional `forever` block to target the alien spaceship and zap it with virtual lasers.

Create the new `forever` block, but do not delete the existing ones. MakeCode features parallelism, allowing you to have more than one `forever` block running simultaneously! This lets the code for the alien and your defenses run at the same time.

Remember to make a new variable, **ray**

Read the code and see if you understand it.

Download the new code to the micro:bit.

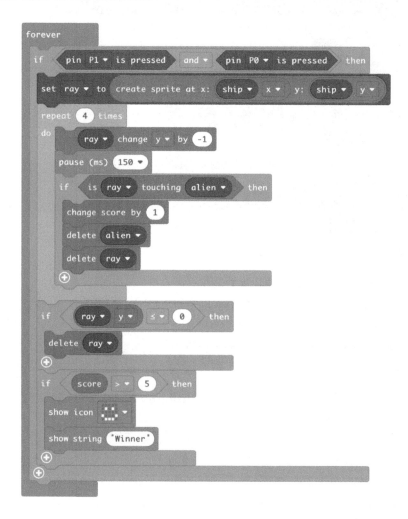

Understanding the code - Zap the alien

Your program should now include two forever blocks.

If the human player presses both the left and right buttons, the ship will fire from the current position upward towards the sky.

The ray sprite is created at the position of the ship. So it appears that the ray comes from the ship. The ray is simulated by the LED going upward four times.

If you hit the alien, you earn a point and both the alien and your projectile disappear.

When your projectile reaches the top of the display, it is deleted.

Score five points and you win the game!

When your game is finished, the complete code should look like this.

```
on start
    set ship ▾ to create sprite at x: 2 y: 4
    set score 0
```

```
on pin P0 ▾ pressed
    ship ▾ change x ▾ by -1
```

```
on pin P1 ▾ pressed
    ship ▾ change x ▾ by 1
```

```
forever
    set alien ▾ to create sprite at x: pick random 0 to 4 y: 0
    pause (ms) 150 ▾
    repeat 4 times
    do
        alien ▾ change y ▾ by 1
        pause (ms) 500 ▾
        if is alien ▾ touching ship ▾ then
            game over
    if is alien ▾ touching edge then
        delete alien ▾
```

```
forever
    if pin P1 ▾ is pressed and ▾ pin P0 ▾ is pressed then
        set ray ▾ to create sprite at x: ship ▾ x ▾ y: ship ▾ y ▾
        repeat 4 times
        do
            ray ▾ change y ▾ by -1
            pause (ms) 150 ▾
            if is ray ▾ touching alien ▾ then
                change score by 1
                delete alien ▾
                delete ray ▾
        if ray ▾ y ▾ ≤ ▾ 0 then
            delete ray ▾
        if score > ▾ 5 then
            show icon
            show string "Winner"
```

Tips

- You can hide the Simulator temporarily using the gray arrow tab on the right edge of the Simulator area. This provides more room for blocks and is useful for larger programs. You can unhide the Simulator to test your work at any time.
- In the game blocks, remember to change the default sprite to your named variable sprites.
- Some of these blocks have complex constructions. Use the colors and shapes to figure out how to build them. In some cases, you may have to look at the drop-down list of options to find the right blocks.

Challenges

- Can you change this game to use the shake left and right instead of the buttons?
- Can you add 5 lives as a variable, so you don't lose the game when the alien touches the bottom?
- If you have a micro:bit V2, can you add sound effects without sacrificing game play?

Fun Fact

This project recreates a micro:bit version of the popular 1978 arcade game, Space Invaders, which itself was based on Breakout, created earlier in the 1970s.

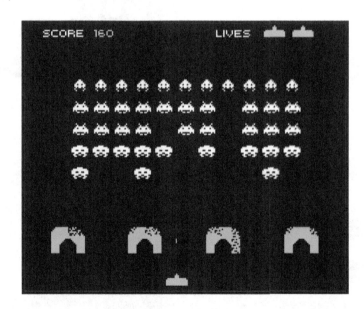

Space Invaders by Tomohiro Nishikado

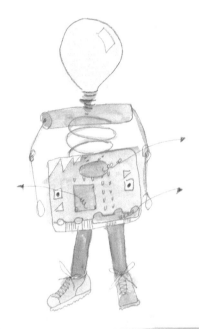

Doctor Shaky

Let's make a Doctor Shaky game out of a shoebox, aluminum foil, and alligator clips. To play the game, you "operate" on the micro:bit-powered patient and remove three items before your time is up. Of course, you can invent your own patient design.

Fun fact: In the Netherlands, the popular game Operation is called Dokter Bibber, which means Doctor Shaky!

Materials
micro:bit, USB cable & 1 battery box, 6 alligator clips, 1 piezo speaker, 1 LED, a shoebox, aluminum foil, tape, scissors, glue or hot glue gun, markers, cardstock, Dr. Shaky template (or your own drawing).

Note: if you are using a micro:bit V2, you may skip adding the speaker.

Template
Use the *Doctor Shaky* template or make your own. Find this downloadable template file at microbit.inventtolearn.com.

Make

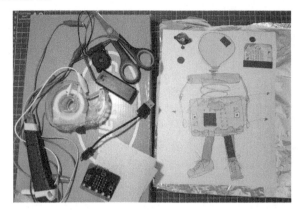

1. Assemble your materials.

2. Put the Dr. Shaky template on the shoebox lid. Don't glue it yet. Cut the indicated holes through the template and lid for the piezo, LED, battery cable and micro:bit connections. Cut three more holes in the patient body area using the template.

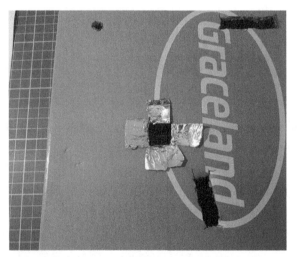

3. Cover the edges of the three patient holes with aluminum foil and tape the edges of the foil on both sides of the box lid.

4. Flip the shoebox lid over. Cut three small pieces of cardstock, each slightly longer and wider than the holes.

5. Fold the cardstock into three small paper boxes to hold small objects underneath the holes in your patient. Tape these boxes in place.

6. Make 3 balls of aluminum foil to pick out the micro:bit robot patient.

7. Remove the template and cover the top of the shoebox lid with aluminum foil. The foil needs to be big enough to wrap around the top edge of the lid. It should cover the holes for the patient, but not the holes for the cables, piezo, or LED.

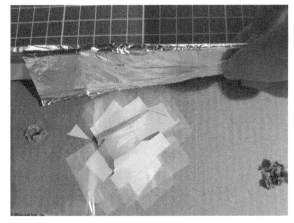

8. Wrap the foil around the edge of the lid. This foil is the ground of the circuit.

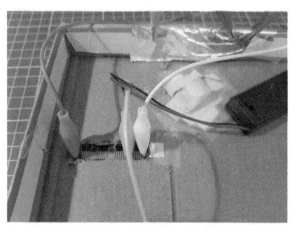

9. Put the template back on the shoebox lid over the aluminum foil. Open all the holes through the foil. Feed the piezo wires through the lid. Before you place the LED in the lid, test it by connecting it to the 3V and GND pins of the powered micro:bit.

10. Attach three alligator clips from underneath the box lid to the micro:bit: 1 clip from GND to the aluminum foil; 1 clip from P0 to one wire of the piezo speaker; and 1 clip from P1 to the long positive leg of the LED.

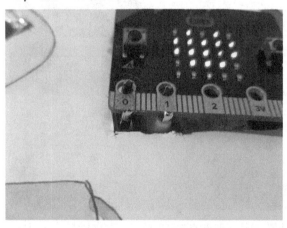

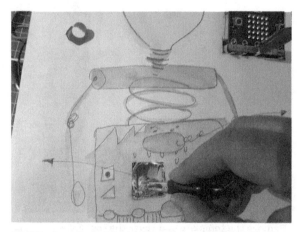

11. Ground the rest of the circuit using the aluminum foil. Attach one clip from the remaining wire of the piezo speaker to the aluminum foil. Attach one clip from the negative shorter leg of the LED to the aluminum foil.

12. Attach a clip to P2. Use the other end of this alligator clip to remove the pieces from the robot. Download the code to your micro:bit and test the game.

Tips

- If the little boxes underneath each patient hole are too big, you will not able to grab your game pieces with the alligator clip.
- If you use non-conductive objects instead of aluminum foil balls, the game will be easier because it will only trigger the game if the metal jaw of the alligator clip touches the side of a hole.
- The large piece of aluminum foil makes it easier to attach all the ground clips to ground. This is similar to using the coin as a shared point of contact in previous projects.

The Invent to Learn Guide to the micro:bit

Connections

The piezo speaker must be attached to pin P0. All music blocks use P0 as the output for music.

Connect the LED to pin P1.

Connect the alligator clip used to grab items from the patient's body to pin P2.

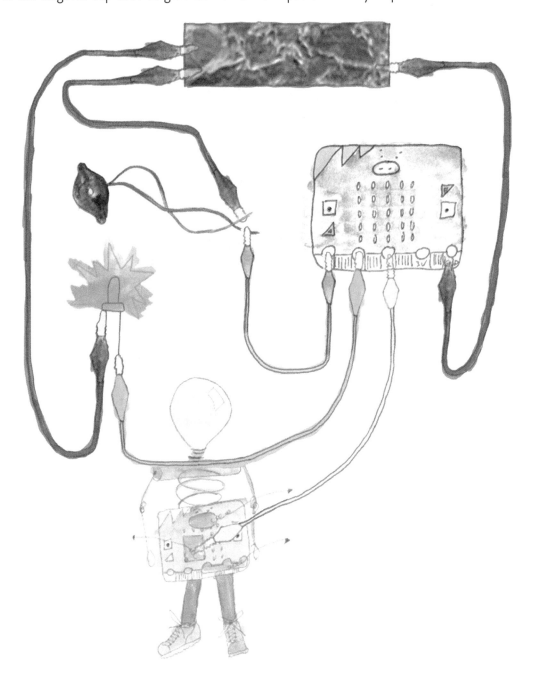

Programming

The object of the game is to remove all the objects from the patient's body without touching the sides of the holes. If the object does touch the aluminum foil around the holes, the LED lights up, a fail icon displays on the micro:bit, and it plays a sound. This first bit of code tests that process.

- Create the following blocks in MakeCode
- Download the code to your micro:bit
- Test the code and debug if necessary

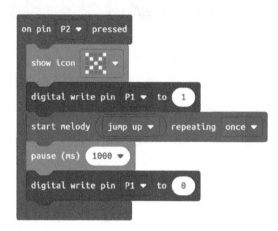

Understanding the code

When the program starts, it displays a heart icon to show that the program is running.

The alligator clip connected to pin P2 is used to grab the objects in the holes in the patient body. If the object is removed without touching the aluminum sides of the hole, nothing happens. But if the metal jaws of the clip or the foil ball touch the sides of the hole, the circuit connecting pin P2 to GND is completed. This triggers the `on pin P2 pressed` event block and all the code inside that block starts to run.

The following things happen:

- Display an X icon
- Light the LED (connected to pin P1)
- Play a sound effect (speaker connected to pin P0)
- Pause 1000 milliseconds (1 second)
- Turn off the LED

Tip

- If the code does not work as expected, try touching the alligator clip directly from pin P2 to GND. This temporarily bypasses the patient and all the extra connections. This is a troubleshooting technique called "isolating the problem."

Programming – A better game

Improve the game by keeping score and limiting the number of tries a player gets within a set period of time before the game is over.

Use the built-in variable blocks found under **Advanced – Game** to keep track of elapsed time, lives, and score. The game blocks know that when all lives are lost, the game is over.

Players have 50,000 ms (50 seconds) to play the game. If they touch the sides of a hole four times, the game is over. Each time they successfully remove an object from the patient, press the A button to record the score. Remove three objects and win!

- Create this program in MakeCode
- Download the code to your micro:bit
- Read the code and see if you understand it
- Test the game and debug if necessary

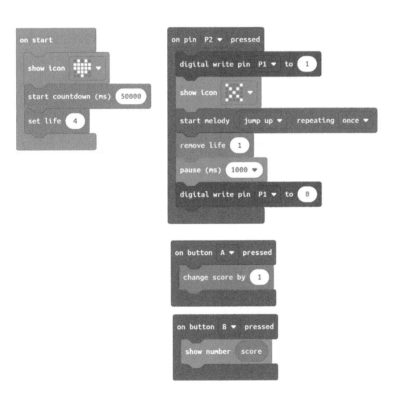
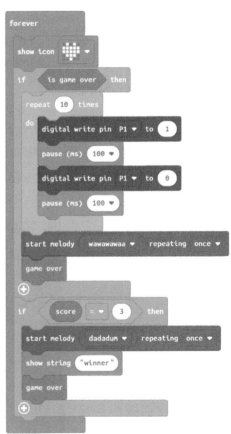

Understanding the code – A better game

`on start` sets a countdown timer to 50 seconds and sets the number of lives a player has to four.

`on pin P2 pressed` works just like it did in the previous code, but this time it removes one life when you touch the sides of a hole.

`on button A` increases your score after removing an object successfully.

`on button B` is a way to check your current score

The `forever` block does all of the heavy lifting in this code.

It shows a heart icon on the micro:bit display.

Then it checks to see if the game is over (when the life game variable goes to zero, the logic block `is game over` becomes **true**). If it is over, the LED flashes ten times, a sad melody is played, and the game is finished.

The `game over` block displays a Game Over animation on the micro:bit.

If the game is not over, the `forever` block checks to see if the player's score equals three. If it is, you have removed all of the objects safely and quickly enough to win the game and are congratulated by music, text, and the game over animation.

Commenting on code

When you write complicated programs, or you work on the code with other people, it is important to add comments to your program. This helps you and others better understand what is happening or may be used to remind you to fix something.

MakeCode makes it easy for you to get into the habit of including comments in your code.

Right mouse click (on a Mac, use control-click) on a block and select **Add Comment.**

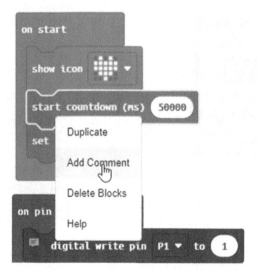

Write your comment and close the block.

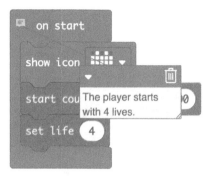

Blocks containing comments gain a little icon to indicate an attached comment. Click to reveal the comment.

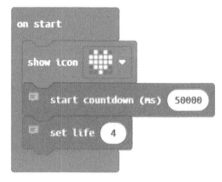

Challenges

- Add more items to be removed from the patient.
- Automatically keep score.
- Make the game easier or harder to play by changing the countdown timer.
- Can you add an animation when you remove an item safely?

A Spooky Game in Scratch

MakeCode is not the only language used to program the micro:bit. There are lots of other options, like Scratch. Since you may already be familiar with Scratch, adding a micro:bit to Scratch projects can be easy and fun. Scratch does not use all of the functionality of the micro:bit. For example, radio communication is not supported. However, there are several benefits of coding the micro:bit with Scratch.

- It's easy to do.
- The micro:bit communicates with the computer wirelessly via Bluetooth. Once a special Scratch hex file is loaded on the micro:bit, no USB cable or downloading is necessary, even when you change your code. The new code will immediately start to run on the micro:bit.
- Your micro:bit code is saved in the Scratch project on your computer, not on the micro:bit. So, you must have the Scratch program running in order to control the micro:bit.
- Your projects may include action on the screen and in physical space. You can use the micro:bit to control animation, storytelling, information display, and more on the computer screen.

Materials

micro:bit, USB cable, battery pack, a computer with internet access and Bluetooth, Scratch Link utility software installed on your computer, a special .hex file that allows your micro:bit to work with Scratch.

Check the requirements for your computer operating system and browser at scratch.mit.edu/microbit

Make

1. Go to scratch.mit.edu/microbit. Follow the instructions to download and install Scratch Link and the special .hex file you will copy to the micro:bit.

2. Download and install **Scratch Link** on your computer.

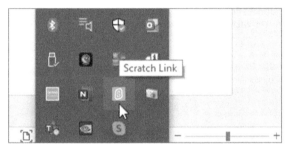

3. Run **Scratch Link**. You should see it running in the toolbar of your computer.

Scratch Link is a small piece of software that allows your computer to communicate between Scratch and the micro:bit wirelessly via Bluetooth.

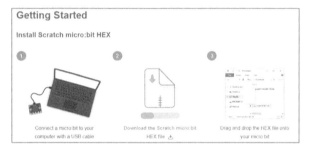

4. Connect the micro:bit to your computer, download the special .hex file and unzip this file (if necessary). Copy the file to the micro:bit. (The micro:bit should appear as a drive on your computer.)

5. Make sure your computer has Bluetooth turned on.

6. Go to scratch.mit.edu and select **Create** or login to your Scratch account.

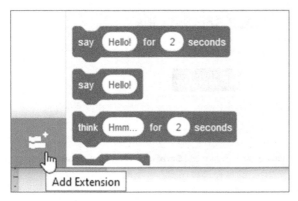

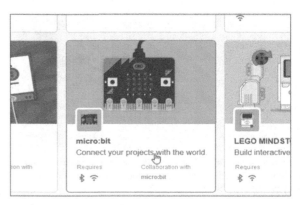

7. Click on the **Add Extension** button at the bottom of the Scratch window.

8. Select micro:bit. Make sure that your micro:bit is on and connected to a battery pack or is connected to your computer with a USB cable.

9. When Bluetooth is on and **Scratch Link** is running, Scratch will look for your micro:bit.

10. The unique name of your micro:bit (a random word) should appear on your micro:bit display. If it does not appear, make sure you copied the Scratch .hex file to it.

When the computer finds your micro:bit, its name should appear on the screen.

Click the **Connect** button.

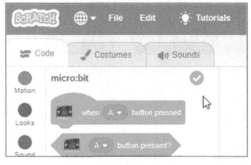

11. Return to the Scratch editor.

12. You should see a new palette of green micro:bit blocks and a green checkmark indicating that everything is working and you are ready to code.

Tips

- You can only connect one micro:bit to each computer running Scratch.
- If you have another browser window or browser tab running Scratch, you should close that one before beginning to program the micro:bit.
- Sometimes Bluetooth is a bit tricky to get working. Open and close your browser, turn Bluetooth on and off, and try **Scratch Link** again.
- Additional troubleshooting tips can be found on the Scratch website. scratch.mit.edu/microbit

Programming with Scratch

Use the micro:bit to control a simple animation on the computer screen by programming the ghost sprite and the skeleton sprite. Pressing the A button will make ghost sounds, pressing B will cause the ghost to fly around the computer screen, and tilting the micro:bit will make the skeleton walk across the screen.

- Remove Sprite1 (the Cat) from the stage
- Create two new sprites and name them ghost and skeleton
- Choose a ghost shape for the ghost sprite and skeleton shape for the skeleton sprite by selecting each sprite and then clicking on the **Choose a Sprite** button (the one that looks like a cat)
- Add a scary forest backdrop to the stage by clicking on the **Choose a Backdrop** button and choosing Woods
- Of course, you may select other sprites and backgrounds or design your own!

Programming – Ghost

- Click on the ghost sprite and create the following program in Scratch.
- Be sure that your micro:bit is connected to your computer.
- Read the program and see if you can make sense of it.
- Click on the green flag at the top of the Scratch screen to put the sprite at the center of the screen.
- Press the A button to make sounds or the B button to make the ghost fly.

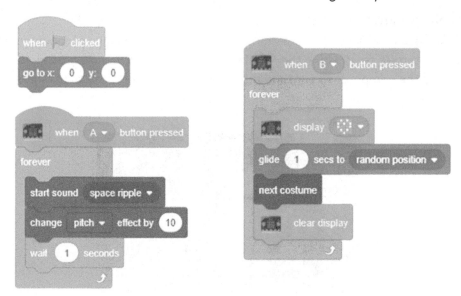

Understanding the code – Ghost

Scratch programs typically run based on an event, like a key press, clicking on the green flag, or moving the micro:bit. In this case, clicking the green flag sends the ghost to the center of the screen [0 0]. Each sprite may be triggered by the same or different events and then run specific instructions based on that event.

When you press the micro:bit A button, a `forever` loop begins.

- Play the space ripple sound and increase its pitch effect each time by 10.
- The computer waits one second and repeats the process.

When the micro:bit B button is pressed, a `forever` loop is started. Inside the loop are instructions to:

- Display a heart icon on the micro:bit.
- Glide for one second to a random position on the screen, change the sprite to the next ghost costume, and clear the micro:bit display.

Programming – Skeleton

Next, program the skeleton sprite. In Scratch, every sprite can have its own set of code blocks.

- Click on the skeleton sprite and create the following program.
- Read the program and try to understand what it does.
- Click on the green flag.
- Tilt the micro:bit side to side and click the B button.

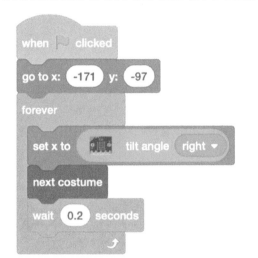
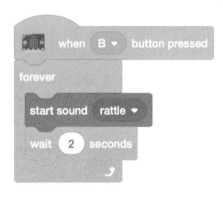

Understanding the code – Skeleton

When the green flag is clicked, the skeleton sprite moves to [-171 -97]. You may of course change these coordinates if you prefer a different starting position.

Start a `forever` loop:

- Slide the sprite along the X axis as the user tilts the micro:bit to the right.
- Flip to the next skeleton costume to produce the illusion of animation.
- Wait .2 seconds (2/10ths of a second).

When the B button is pressed, trigger a `forever` block that starts the sound, **rattle**, then waits 2 seconds.

Tip

- A version of this Scratch project may be found at scratch.mit.edu/projects/413444215

Challenges

- Use different sounds in your project.
- Use different sprite costumes or paint your own.
- Program something to happen if the A and B buttons are both pressed on the micro:bit.

More inspiration for Scratch and micro:bit projects

The Scratch page on the micro:bit website has downloadable and printable cards that work well as quick project starters. microbit.org/scratch

The Make It: Code It page on the micro:bit website has step-by-step sample projects for Scratch and the micro:bit. microbit.org/projects/make-it-code-it/

The micro:bit page on the Scratch website includes starter projects, getting started printable cards, and troubleshooting tips. scratch.mit.edu/microbit

A Scratch Studio collection of micro:bit projects can be found at scratch.mit.edu/studios/5812900

Another way to find ideas for micro:bit and Scratch projects is to search for "micro:bit" while on the Scratch website. You might also search for "microbit" (without the colon) to find others. From there, you can remix another user's project or just borrow programming ideas from them.

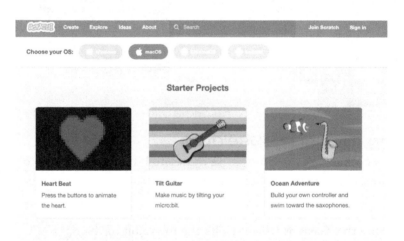

Scratch Teacher Tips

Using Scratch with the micro:bit offers some interesting project options that MakeCode does not. Since Scratch controls both the action on the micro:bit and the computer screen, you can use the micro:bit to control screen action or sounds. For example, see the *Race Car Game Controller in Scratch* project in this book. However, Scratch does not use all the features of the micro:bit, such as radio or many of the sensors.

- Scratch uses a different operating system on the micro:bit than MakeCode. This is the reason you must copy a special Scratch .hex file to the micro:bit in order for it to communicate with Scratch. You can use either Scratch or MakeCode on a micro:bit, but not both at the same time.
- To return to programming in MakeCode after using Scratch, just download any MakeCode program to the micro:bit. MakeCode files include the code and the operating system. Therefore, when you download a MakeCode project to the micro:bit configured for Scratch, it will immediately start to run the MakeCode program on the micro:bit. Since this is a larger than normal file, it might take a bit longer to download. Be patient. To return to running Scratch programs, you must go through the entire initialization process and reinstall the Scratch .hex file onto the micro:bit.
- Be sure to download and use the latest version of the Scratch Link software.
- Check that your classroom computers are updated to the required operating systems and browsers. Review the requirements at scratch.mit.edu/microbit
- You might wish to have students begin working with the micro:bit and Scratch, and then move on to MakeCode. Or have younger students use Scratch and older students using MakeCode.
- If you have multiple classes or groups of students using MakeCode and some using Scratch, it might a good idea to configure a bunch of micro:bits to work with Scratch and keep those separate from the ones being used with MakeCode or another programming language. This will save time having to reconfigure Scratch every time students want to use it.
- In a classroom setting, Bluetooth connections may conflict with one another. Ask students to spread out as they work on projects.
- Scratch programs for the micro:bit run on the computer, not on the micro:bit. So, the micro:bit will stop running the program if the computer is closed, the Scratch program is stopped, or the browser is closed.
- Download and print the project starter cards from the micro:bit Scratch website to have on hand for students who want to work on an independent project (microbit.org/scratch).
- For additional resources about teaching with Scratch, the Graduate School of Education at Harvard University maintains an archived ScratchEd website with resources and articles for educators (scratched.gse.harvard.edu). They also support a meetup.com group for Scratch educators (meetup.com/pro/scratched) and a Facebook page (facebook.com/groups/TeachingwithScratch).

Let's Get Physical

Halloween
— 113 —

Art Machine
— 118 —

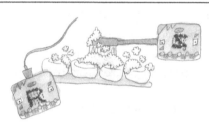

Smart Toothbrush
— 123 —

Extend MakeCode with Your Own Functions
— 126 —

Nightlight
— 131 —

Race Car Controller in Scratch
— 142 —

Halloween

Bring a carved pumpkin to life with some battery-operated holiday lights and spooky sounds. A flickering effect is created with animation on a micro:bit placed inside the pumpkin. Add a second micro:bit to control the jack-o'-lantern remotely!

Materials

micro:bit, USB cable & battery pack, 2 alligator clips, zipper plastic bag, cutting knife, pumpkin, battery-powered holiday lights, scissors, small (battery-powered) speaker, tape, wire stripper.

Note: if you are using a micro:bit V2, you may skip adding the speaker, but an external speaker might be louder.

Caution! The micro:bit will be damaged permanently if it gets wet. It's always a good idea to keep electronics dry.

Make

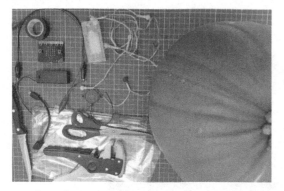

1. Collect all your materials.

2. Safely carve your Halloween pumpkin.

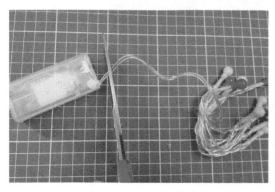

3. Cut the wire of the holiday lights just before the battery pack.

4. Strip one inch of insulation off each wire connected to the lights. A wire stripper is the safest and easiest tool for doing this.

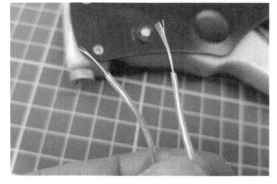

5. The wires should look like this.

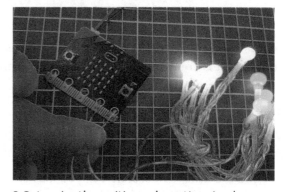

6. Determine the positive and negative wires by connecting the wires to 3V and GND on the micro:bit. If they do not light, reverse the wires. Be sure the micro:bit is powered for this test. Label the wires with a + and -.

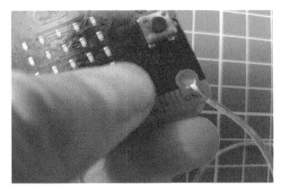

7. Wrap the negative wire of the holiday lights around the GND pin and secure with an alligator clip.

8. Connect the positive wire of the holiday lights to pin P1 and tape it down firmly. Connect an alligator clip to pin P0 for your speaker.

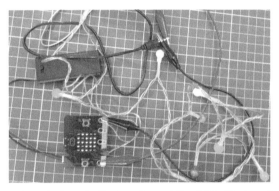

9. Attach the P0 alligator clip and the GND alligator clip to the plug for your speaker (like in *Jingle Bells* project).

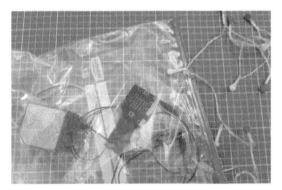

10. Test your code on the micro:bit, disconnect it from the computer, and plug the battery pack into the micro:bit. To protect your micro:bit, wrap everything except the lights in a zipper plastic bag.

11. Place the plastic bag with your micro:bit and speaker in your pumpkin. Distribute the lights around the inside of the pumpkin.

12. Your project is done. Turn on your spooky jack-o'-lantern!

Connections

The speaker is connected to pin P0 and GND. The positive wire of the holiday lights is taped to P1. The negative wire of the holiday lights is connected to GND.

The micro:bit, battery pack, and speaker should be in a tightly closed plastic bag before being placed in the pumpkin.

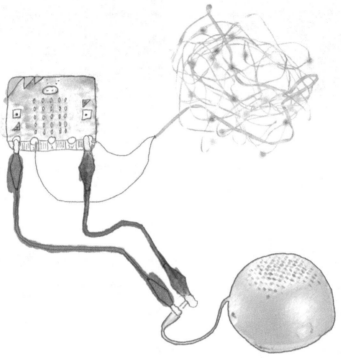

Programming

- Create the code
- Test it in the Simulator
- Save the project with a filename like *Halloween*
- Download the code to the micro:bit

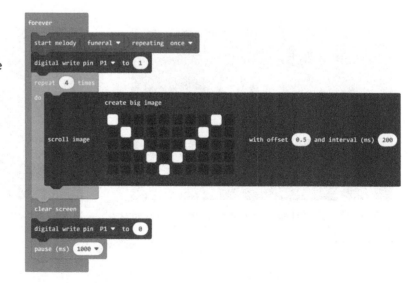

Understanding the code

In a `forever` loop, repeat the following instructions:

- The `start melody repeating` block tells the micro:bit to play the funeral melody one time.
- The first `digital write pin` block sends power to P1 which turns the string of lights on.
- Scroll a wave across the micro:bit screen four times. The two Image blocks you need are found in the **Images** panel in the **Advanced** section of the Toolkit. `create big image` needs to be dragged inside of the `scroll image` block. The offset and interval settings control the movement and speed of the scroll. This image scrolls on the micro:bit LEDs and does not change anything on the string of lights.
- Clear the screen.
- The second `digital write pin` turns off the power to pin P1. That turns the lights off.
- Wait one second before running the sequence again within the forever loop.

Add a remote control

This version of the code adds a second micro:bit as a remote control to trigger the jack-o'-lantern to come alive and then go back to sleep.

To add a remote control, use this code as a replacement for the program we just created.

Drag the blocks that were inside the `forever` block into an `on radio received` block. The `forever` block should now be empty and may be deleted. This changes the jack-o'-lantern from one that sings and flashes forever to one that turns on only when triggered by the remote control. Now it only repeats the action four times.

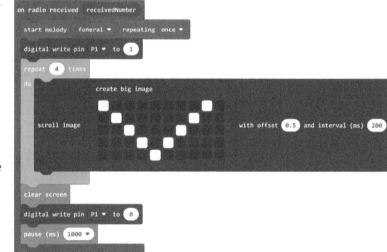

Be sure to download the code to **both** micro:bits, the one connected to the lights and the one being used as a remote control!

Challenges

- Compose a new melody or sound effects.
- Use the B button to make different sounds or to make the lights behave differently.
- Add a second set of different colored lights to the project and turn those on by pressing the B button on the remote micro:bit.

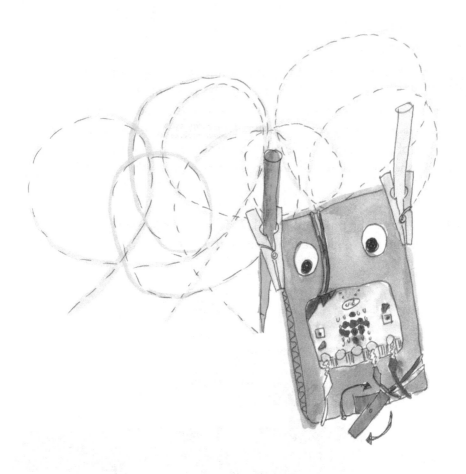

Art Machine

Turn a micro:bit into an abstract artist with pencils and a continuous 360-degree servo motor. As your machine moves, it draws!

The servos we have used in previous projects rotate between 0 and 180 degrees like a garage door or windshield wipers. This servo rotates 360 degrees like a wheel turns and propels the Art Machine to move in response to a flashlight.

Materials

micro:bit, USB cable & battery pack, 1 continuous (360) servo motor, 3 male alligator cables, 2 pencils or markers, a stiff piece of cardboard, 2 clothespins, hot glue gun, paper, wobbly eyes, scissors, tape, 2 pieces of Velcro, popsicle stick, and a sheet (or two) of paper.

Make

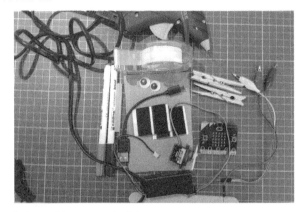

1. Assemble your materials.

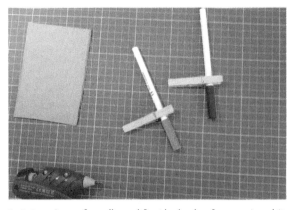

2. Cut a piece of cardboard for the body of your micro:bit artist. Put a marker in each of the clothespins.

3. Add a little bit of hot glue to the side of each clothespin, taking care not to get glue on the markers.

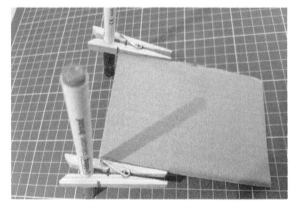

4. Glue them to the sides of the cardboard as shown.

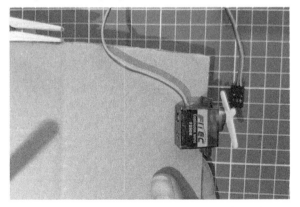

5. Glue the servo motor to the top of the cardboard.

6. Hot glue a piece of popsicle stick on the servo motor or attach it with a screw.

7. Attach the battery and the micro:bit with some Velcro and add the googly eyes. The battery can go on the bottom of the cardboard.

8. Attach the cable's between the servo motor and the micro:bit. See the Connections diagram.

9. Place the pencils or markers on a sheet of white paper.

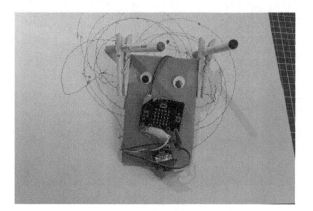

10. Use a flashlight or cellphone light to control the micro:bit.

Tips

- Connect the clothespins with hot glue or tape.
- Tape the cables to the bottom of your machine so they don't drag.
- Use a large piece of white paper as your art canvas.

Connections

This diagram shows how to connect the male alligator cables between the servo motor and the micro:bit. The dark cable on the servo motor connects to GND, the red cable on the servo connects to 3V, and the orange cable connects to P0, P1, or P2.

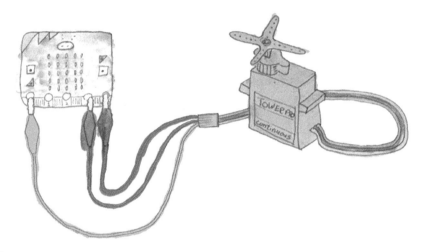

Programming

To program the continuous servo motor, use the servo blocks from the **Extensions** section of the Toolbox. Continuous servo blocks set the speed of the motor from 0% (off) to 100% (full speed).

- Create this program in MakeCode.
- Read the code and predict how it will behave.
- Save and download the program to your micro:bit.
- Point a flashlight at the micro:bit and see if the robot artist draws. Adjust your machine as necessary.
- You may use the MakeCode Simulator to test your code. Change the light level with your mouse and observe the simulated light level bar graph and servo motion.

Understanding the code

There is no dedicated light sensor on the micro:bit. A bit of technical wizardry is used to turn the LEDs of the micro:bit display into a sensor for measuring light.

Start the program by displaying a smiley face.

A loop runs and constantly checks the amount of light received by the light sensor (the LEDs in the micro:bit display). This will be a number from 0 to 255.

While the light level is higher than the ambient light in the room, set the speed of the servo motor to the current light level. More light makes the motor spin faster.

Try different values as substitutes for 100 in the `while` block to make the robot artist move only when a light is shining on it, not all the time.

Be sure that the continuous servo block is set to the pin where the alligator clip connects the servo to the micro:bit.

Display the light level as a bar graph on the micro:bit display.

Otherwise, stop the servo and clear the display screen.

Challenges

- Make your micro:bit sturdier by using a piece of wood instead of cardboard.
- Use paint brushes instead of markers or pencils.
- Can you make your robot artist start and stop with a remote?
- Can you program your robot to draw straight lines of equal lengths?
- Decorate your art machine.

Smart Toothbrush

Let's make a simple game to encourage two minutes of vigorous tooth brushing!

Materials

1 micro:bit, 1 battery pack, USB cable, toothbrush, scissors, 2 pieces of Velcro, cardboard or felt.

Make

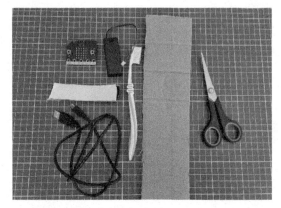

1. Collect your materials.

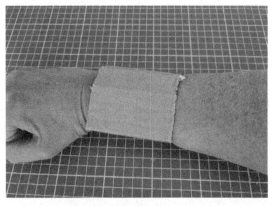

2. Fit the cardboard around your wrist.

3. Put Velcro tape on the end of the cardboard, so you can take your cardboard bracelet on and off. Attach the micro:bit and the battery pack.

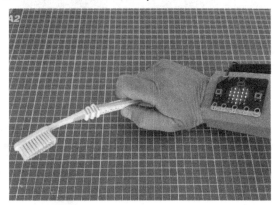

4. Download the code to the micro:bit and test the toothbrush game.

Tips

- Be careful! The micro:bit should not get wet!
- You may also use felt or other material to use as a bracelet around your wrist.
- Of course, you can test the timer by just shaking your hand.

Programming

- Create the following code. The dark green **Game** blocks are in the **Advanced** section of the Toolbox.
- Download the program to your micro:bit
- Press the A button to begin
- Brush your teeth!

Understanding the code

The code for the project seems simple but the **Game** blocks do a lot of work in the background.

- A toothy icon appears when the micro:bit starts and the game's score will be initialized to zero.
- When you press the A button, the `start countdown` block starts a timer and plays an animation. Making a tooth brushing motion causes the score to increase by 1. Every score change plays a quick animation on the micro:bit display.
- The `on 3g` block checks for 3g or more worth of force being sensed by the shaken micro:bit. You can also try using `on 6g` or `on shake`.
- When time runs out, an animation is played followed by a scrolling "Game Over" message and the final score is displayed.
- The game ends after 2 minutes (120,000 ms). You might test the program by shortening the length of the game by reducing the amount of time being counted down. Try 5,000 ms, for example.
- The `reset` block resets the micro:bit and the program starts over. You could also press the reset button on the back of the micro:bit board to start the game over, but this is a way to start over under program control.
- The `reset` block is found in the **Advanced** section of the Toolbox under **Control.**

Make your game better

- Is there a way a player can lose?
- Add sound to your game if you are using a micro:bit V2
- Can you add a "time running out" signal to your game?

Challenges

- Modify the game to work when jumping rope or bouncing on a trampoline.
- Can you attach a micro:bit to a skateboard to record jumps?
- Think about how you might use the `on 8g` block.

Extend MakeCode with Your Own Functions

MakeCode allows you to build your own blocks. Those blocks, called functions, come in especially handy when your programs become longer or more complicated. This project provides some practice programming with functions and does not require you to build anything.

Materials

micro:bit, USB cable.

MakeCode functions

A MakeCode function is like adding your own blocks to a project. Functions are especially useful when the same code is used repeatedly in a program. They add blocks to your programming vocabulary and may be created to act like any type of block built into MakeCode.

Once you define a function, you "call" it in your program to run.

User-created functions are saved with your MakeCode project. These new blocks do not become a permanent part of the MakeCode environment.

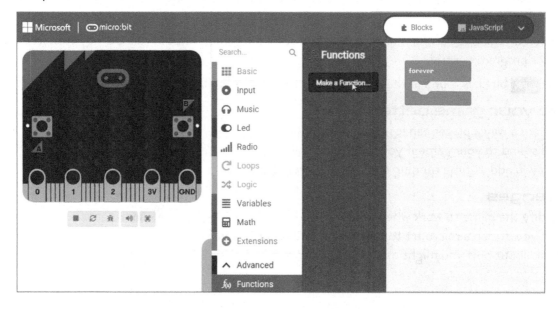

Make a function

Open **Functions** under **Advanced** in the Toolbox.

Make a function by clicking on the **Make a Function** button.

Change the name of the function by typing a new name in the field at the top of the block and click **Done**. Your function will appear in the Workspace.

You may also change the name of the function once the block appears in the MakeCode Workspace.

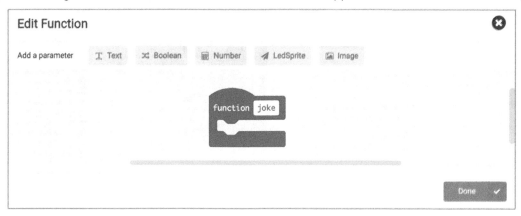

Define your function

Add blocks to the new joke function block to define its behavior like in the following example.

When you define a new function, MakeCode automatically creates a `call` block to run that function.

Add `call joke` to an `on start` block and download the code. Your micro:bit now knows how to tell a joke.

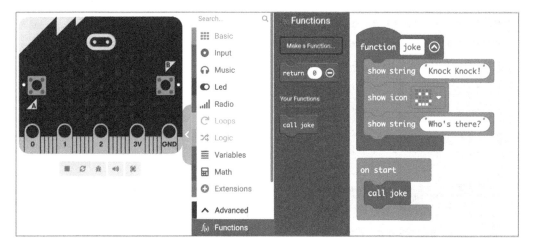

Functions in action

Now that you know how to create a new function, let's do something with them.

- Create a new project and name it something like *Function fun*.
- Create the following blocks, including two new functions with silly names.
- Read the code and see if you understand it.
- Download the code to the micro:bit.
- Press the A or B button and see how they call the functions you defined.

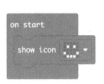  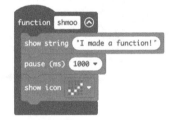 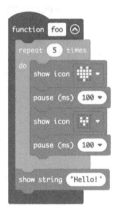

Understanding functions

Function names are arbitrary. A person's name does not tell you much about that person. A function's name is quite similar, it is merely a name associated with a sequence of instructions. We use silly names here to reinforce that point. You of course should name functions in meaningful ways that help you remember their role.

The **shmoo** function displays some text, pauses one second, and shows a check mark icon.

The **foo** function creates a repeating animation and then says, "Hello!"

When the A or B buttons are pressed, one of the two functions will be called to run.

You may collapse a function block by clicking on the arrow in the circle at the top of the block. This just cleans up your workspace a bit. Click the same button to expand the function to see its contents.

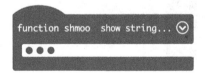 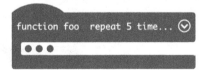

Programming - Gym class

Let's make more functions. Create a **jump** function to display an animation.

Next, create a slightly more complex function, called **exercise**. This function will have a variable input.

Do this by making a function with the name, **exercise**, but before leaving the **Edit Function** window, click on the number button. 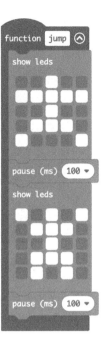 Number

Things should now look like this. **num** is now an input, also called a parameter, of the function. In this case, it gives the function a numerical input that you can control.

Change the parameter name from **num** to **times** and click **Done**. It's a good idea to use parameter names that help us remember what they do.

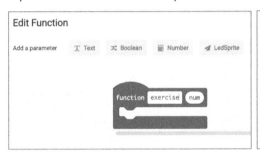 

Define your new exercise function by creating the following block in MakeCode.

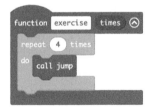

Replace the 4 in the `repeat` block with the parameter, **times**. This works by clicking and dragging just like you did when you used `on radio received` blocks.

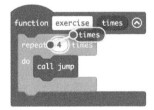

Create the **lazy** and **workout** functions , and add to on button A and on button B blocks so that your program now looks like this.

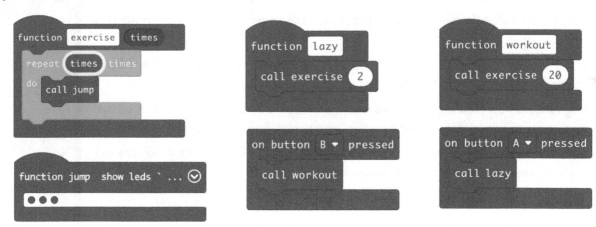

- Save the program with the name of your choice.
- Download the program to the micro:bit.
- Read the code and try to understand what it does.
- Click the A or B buttons on the micro:bit to make the creature on the display exercise.

Understanding the code – Gym class

This project uses functions to call other functions. In other words, new functions can be built using other functions. In some programming languages, these are called procedures and subprocedures, or routines and subroutines.

The **exercise** function calls the **jump** function and repeats **jump** a variable number of times, controlled by the parameter times .

The function **lazy** tells **exercise** to run the animation 2 times.

The **workout** function instructs **exercise** to run the animation 20 times.

The on button A block tells the micro:bit to be lazy and the on button B block causes the micro:bit creature to do 20 jumping jacks.

Tips

- It is a good idea to use single word names for functions. That's why the default names are **dosomething**, **dosomething1**, **dosomething2**, etc.
- Name a function something logical so you can remember what it is supposed to do.

Nightlight

In this project, you will make an automatic nightlight that turns on when the room gets dark. You will also work a bit of craft magic to make translucent paper for the invention.

Materials

micro:bit, USB cable & battery pack, 3 LEDs, aluminum foil, tape, 4 alligator clips, glue (or hot glue gun), olive oil, cardboard, paper, scissors, paper napkin or paper towel, Nightlight template.

Make

1. Gather your materials.

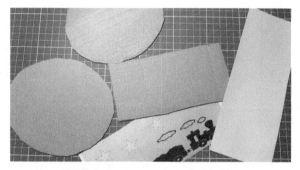

2. Print and cut the template pieces from the template. Cut out two round pieces and one rectangle out of cardboard.

3. Take the printed train template (or a drawing of your own approximately the same size) and use a piece of paper towel or napkin to rub olive oil on it. This makes the paper translucent, allowing light to shine through.

4. Let the olive oil coated paper dry for at least 30 minutes.

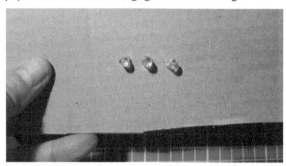

5. Make three holes in the cardboard rectangle and insert the LED lights in a row. Make sure the + and - legs of the LEDs are arranged either at the top or bottom of the row. Remember, the longer legs are positive.

Draw + and - signs on the back of the cardboard to keep track of which row of LED legs is positive and which is negative.

6. Flip the cardboard over and put a piece of aluminum foil behind the - legs of the LEDs. Tape them down on the aluminum foil. Make sure the foil does not touch the + legs of the LEDs.

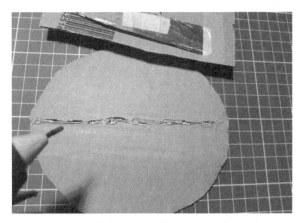

7. Glue the edge of the rectangle onto a circle so that it stands up in the middle of the circle.

8. It should look like this.

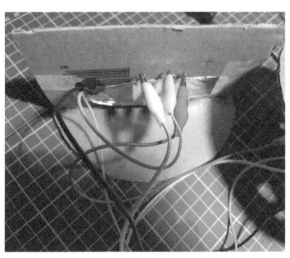

9. On the other side, attach the positive leg of each LED light to an alligator clip. Attach another alligator clip to the aluminum foil. The foil serves as the ground for all three LEDs.

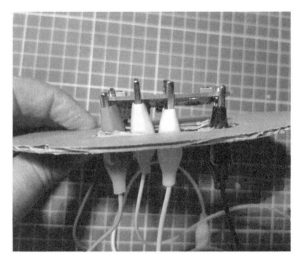

10. Attach the micro:bit to the second cardboard circle with the LED display showing. This will be the top of your nightlight. Take the other ends of the positive alligator clips and poke them through the cardboard so they attach to pins P0, P1, and P2.

Poke the alligator clip attached to the foil through the cardboard and attach to GND.

11. Glue the cardboard circle with the micro:bit to the top of your nightlight. Poke one more hole and feed the battery cable back through the cardboard top. Attach the battery pack to the underside of the top.

12. Tape the paper you coated with olive oil between the top and bottom cardboard circles. Trim it to fit as needed.

13. When it fits, remove the tape and use lots of glue or hot glue to make everything stay together. This may be tricky due to the slippery oil coating.

14. Download the code to your micro:bit and test it by placing your hand above the micro:bit to make the light sensor think the room has become dark.

Template

Use the Nightlight template or make your own. Find this downloadable template file at microbit.inventtolearn.com.

Connections

Look carefully at this diagram to see how the cables and LEDs are connected. The negative legs of the three LEDs are all connected to the aluminum foil, which is connected to the GND pin on the micro:bit. The positive legs of the three LEDs are connected to P0, P1, and P2.

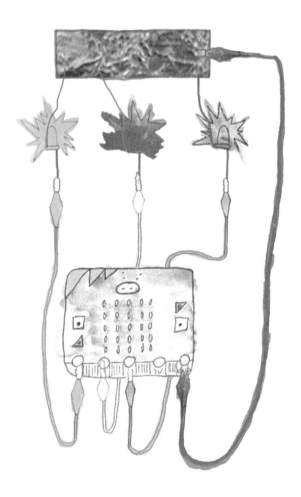

Programming

This project develops in sophistication as we learn a bit more code and build the nightlight.

For the first level of this coding project, you don't even need to build your nightlight. We will just use the display on the micro:bit to provide light and practice using the light sensor much like we used the bar graph block in the *Art Machine* project.

The program for this project is quite simple.

- Create the following code.
- Find the subtraction block under **Math** in the Toolbox.
- Read it and predict what it will do.
- Test it in the Simulator.
- Save the project with a filename like *Nightlight*.
- Download the code to your micro:bit
- Make any modifications you wish.

Understanding the code

A forever loop plots a bar graph of the light level being sensed in the room. The micro:bit light sensor reports a number between 0 (no light) and 255 (most light) as the light level. Plot bar graph creates an image on the 5x5 grid of pixels that grows and shrinks depending on the input, in this case, the light level.

Since this is a nightlight, we want the pixel bar graph to be fully on in the dark, and decrease as the room gets brighter. Subtracting 255 means that a dark room generates a full plot of pixels, and a bright room turns off most of the pixels.

Program – Nightlight

Now let's build the nightlight. LEDs connected to the micro:bit will create more light than the micro:bit display. In this program, your micro:bit still checks the light level in the room and turns on more pixels as the room gets darker. Now the program will not only control the 5x5 grid of pixels on the micro:bit, but will also turn on the external LEDs one at a time.

You should have three LEDs connected to P0, P1, and P2. This program also includes a function you create named *LEDS OFF*. Check the *Extend MakeCode with Your Own Functions* project for a full explanation of functions.

Create the following program in MakeCode

- To create the function *LEDS OFF*, go to **Advanced – Functions** in the Toolbox and click on **Make a Function...** Build and name the function as shown. This creates a new block `call LEDS OFF` in the **Functions** panel.
- Click the **+** sign at the bottom of the **If** block to create additional **If** blocks. Of course, you can just drag a new **If** block out of the Toolbox if you prefer.
- Be sure that three LEDs are connected to the micro:bit.
- Read the program and try to understand what the code is going to do.
- Download your program to the micro:bit.
- Test your invention by changing the amount of light the micro:bit can sense.
- Fix any bugs and download a new version if necessary.

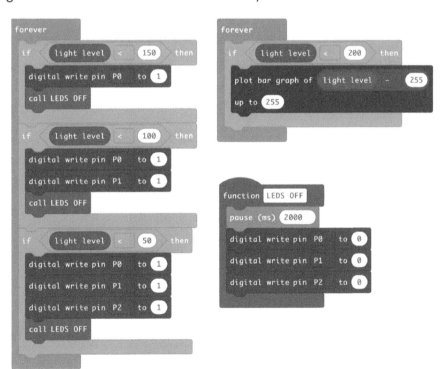

Understanding the code - Nightlight

Two `forever` blocks are running in parallel (simultaneously). One has the job of controlling the external LEDs and the other plots the light level on the micro:bit pixel display.

The longer `forever` block checks the light level in the room read by the micro:bit light sensor. As the light level falls below three different values, LEDs in the nightlight are turned on to illuminate the room.

The `digital write pin` block sends power to a pin when it is set to 1 and cuts the power when it is set to 0. Think of this as on or off.

The new function, *LEDS OFF*, waits 2 seconds and then turn all three LEDs off. Without this function, the same four blocks would have to be used three times in the forever block. By creating a function, your code is simplified.

When the `call LEDS OFF` block is used, the *LEDS OFF* function is called and the three LEDs are turned off after a pause.

If it seems strange to turn the LEDs on, and then have the function turn them off again, remember that the forever block will keep running. If the light level is still low, the LEDS will be immediately turned on again.

Change the length of the pause in the *LEDS OFF* function to suit your taste.

The brightness in the room may vary, so feel free to experiment with the light level threshold values in the logic blocks.

Tip

- The next part of the project is for V2 micro:bits because it uses a sound sensor to turn the Nightlight on and off. As an alternative, V1 micro:bit users could use a second micro:bit as a remote control.

Clap off!

If you have a micro:bit V2, you can use the following program to turn the nightlight off when you clap your hands.

only

Programming the micro:bit - Clap off

Change your existing program to look like the following code.

- Read the code and see if you can predict how it will work.
- Create a new variable named *clap heard* in the **Variables** section of the Toolbox.
- Download the code to the micro:bit.
- Test the program by changing the light level in the room.
- Clap your hands to turn the nightlight off.

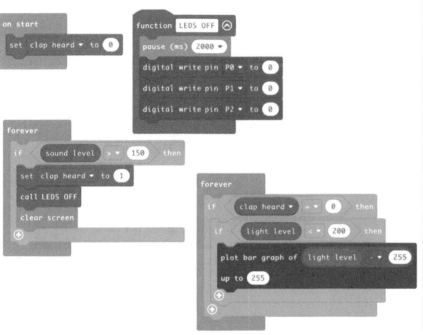

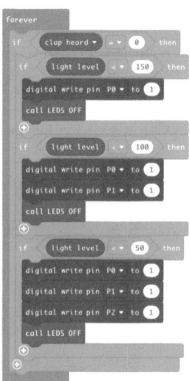

Understanding the code - Clap off

`on start`, set the *clap heard* variable to 0 to set its initial state.

If *clap heard* is set to 0, the nightlight has not heard a clap and performs as before. It lights the LEDs and displays the light level on the micro:bit display.

If the new `forever` block detects that the sound level gets loud, like if it hears a clap, it sets the *clap heard* variable to 1. This tells the display to stop plotting the light level, the *LEDS OFF* function runs to turn off the LEDs, and the micro:bit display is cleared. This is a binary operation, on or off. The nightlight is on until the variable *clap heard* is set to 1.

Clap on! Clap off!

The next version of the code allows you to clap to turn on the nightlight and then turn it off by clapping again. In this case, clapping is like a switch that reverses the current status of your nightlight. Off switches to on and on switches to off.

In this version of the project, we simplify the invention and only use the external LEDs. The bar graph is eliminated.

Programming - Clap on! Clap off!

Change your existing program to look like the following code.

- Read the code and see if you can predict how it will work.
- Create a new variable called *switch is on* in the **Variables** section of the Toolbox. This variable will be either True or False. Find the block in the **Logic** section of the Toolbox.
- Be sure to delete the `forever` block that controls the micro:bit bar graph.
- Download the code to the micro:bit.
- Test the program by changing the light level in the room.
- Clap your hands to turn the nightlight off. Clap again to turn the light on. Repeat.

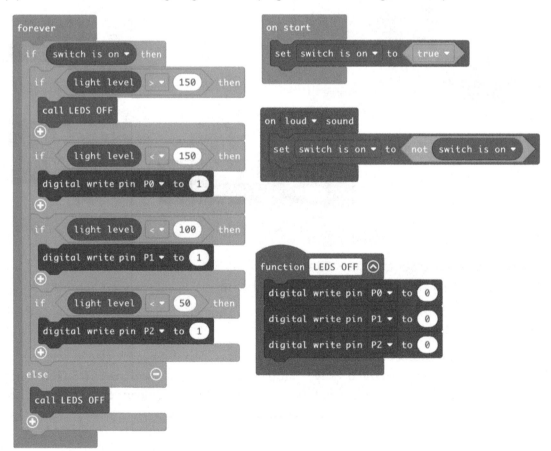

Understanding the code - Clap on! Clap off!

This version of the program works a lot like the previous version except clapping toggles a switch on and off by using an on loud sound event block and a bit of logic.

`on start` initializes the variable `switch is on` by setting its value to *true*.

`on loud sound` tells the micro:bit to listen for a loud sound, such as a clap. When that sound is detected, the variable `switch is on` is set to the opposite of its current state. True becomes false and false becomes true. True and false are used in conditionals (if statements).

Now, the `forever` block checking the light level and turning the LEDs on, checks to see if the current state of `switch is on` is true. Otherwise, the lights are left off.

Challenges

- Design your own illustration to decorate the nightlight.
- Can you program your nightlight to play a lullaby when it gets dark?
- Program your nightlight to turn the bar graph on or off in response to clapping.

Race Car Game Controller in Scratch

In this project you will program a race car video game in Scratch and create an incredible balance board controller powered by the micro:bit.

Using the micro:bit with Scratch was introduced in the *Spooky Game in Scratch* project. Make sure that the micro:bit has the special Scratch.hex file on it and your computer is running the Scratch Link software to make this all work.

To jumpstart your programming, we will start with an existing Scratch project. You may of course modify it and make it better.

Materials
micro:bit, USB cable & battery pack, a computer with internet access and Bluetooth capabilities, a wooden board strong enough to stand on (approximately 20 inches or 50 cm in length), a log or similar round piece of wood, tape or Velcro, 2 screws, screwdriver, 2 small wooden blocks to keep your log in place.

Make

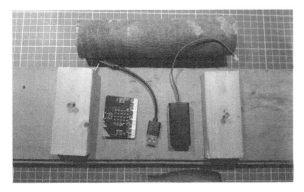

1. Gather your tools and materials.

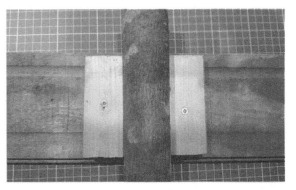

2. Make sure the log fits between your 2 wooden blocks.

3. Screw the 2 small wooden blocks onto the wooden board.

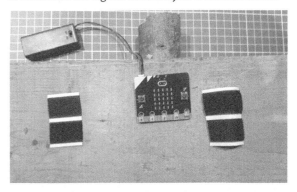

4. Tape or Velcro your micro:bit and battery to the balance board. Position the micro:bit in the center of the top side of the board.

5. You can hide the battery on the underside of the board.

6. Test your balance board by standing on it and rocking side to side. If the movement is too small, make your wooden board shorter.

Tips

- You can play the Scratch/micro:bit game without the balance board by just holding the micro:bit in your hand.
- If you already own a balance board, just attach the micro:bit and battery to it and you're ready to play!
- Feel free to paint or decorate your new controller.

Programming

Follow the instructions at scratch.mit.edu/microbit to set up the Scratch environment for micro:bit programming.

To make things easier in this project, we created a Scratch program for you to edit and improve. Find it at scratch.mit.edu/projects/415030628/. This Scratch project is a remix of a project by @pedbad and @tul1.

Click the **⟨⟩ See Inside** button to edit the Scratch project and make it your own.

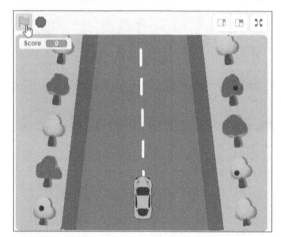

Start the game by clicking on the Green Flag.
You can restart the game by making a sound.

The blue car follows your motion on the balance board!
You can play the game in full screen mode.

You control the blue car with your balance board. Lean to the left and your car will slide left. Lean to the right and your car will slide right. Be careful and take reasonable precautions by clearing enough space around you as you balance on the board.

Understanding the code

Click on the blue car sprite to see these blocks in the code.

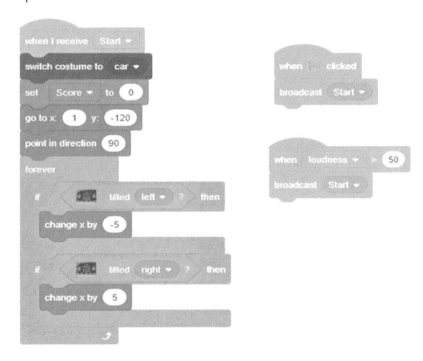

- When the player clicks on the **Green Flag**, broadcast **Start**.
- When the start message is received, the score is set to 0 and a forever loop will begin.
- If the micro:bit is tilted left, change the sprite's x position by -5 and if the micro:bit is tilted right, change x by 5.
- If the game is over, make a sound loud enough to trigger the `when loudness` event which then broadcasts **Start** to play a new game.

Program - Obstacles and special effects

There are additional blocks in the code area of the blue car sprite. They detect whether you hit one of the obstacles (car-2, ball, or thunder) as well as check to see if your car stays on the road. If not, there will be trouble!

A new block `Crash` has been defined and added to Scratch. It works like a MakeCode function. Scratch also lets you create your own blocks.

Read these blocks to understand them.

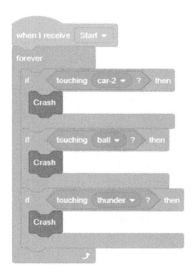
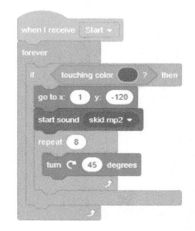

Understanding the code - Obstacles and special effects

When blue car receives the start message, there is another forever loop that checks if it is touching another one of the sprites. If the sprites are touching, the `Crash` function runs.

Another forever loop is triggered when the game starts. This one checks to see if the blue car has run into the edge of the road. If it does, there is a sound and an animation of the car spinning around.

When there is a crash, play a sound and stop the game.

Program – Ball rolling down the street

Click on the ball sprite to see code that makes it appear that a ball is rolling down the street. This creates an illusion of forward motion for the car you're driving. Each time the ball reaches the bottom edge of the screen, you earn one point.

Understanding the code - Ball rolling down the street

When the ball receives the start message it will hide.

Then in a forever loop, the ball waits 2.5 seconds before appearing at the top of the screen (Y = 150) with a random X coordinate between -120 and 120. This randomness makes the game more fun since you have to steer around it.

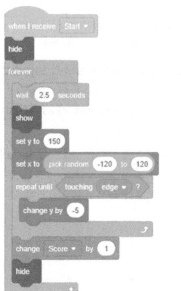

The ball keeps moving down the screen by -5 steps until it hits the bottom edge of the screen.

Then you are awarded 1 point for staying in the race.

Thunder and car-2

The code for thunder and car-2 is almost the same as for the ball except that their starting positions are slightly different . The delay before they appear is also different for each sprite.

Be sure to click on each sprite and read its code to see how it is different from that of the ball.

Challenges

- Can you add more obstacles to your game?
- Make the car go faster the longer the game goes on.
- Change the design of the background or sprites.
- Add a Game Over announcement.
- Create an explosion animation when you crash.
- Can you change the background after 10 points are scored? Or perhaps it turns into night time.
- Can you add music to the game?
- Play your friends' games and make suggestions for improving them.

Here is an example of a similar game, but with different art. Try your balance board controller with it. scratch.mit.edu/projects/466714720

Super-Duper

Wearable Computing
— 149 —

**Talking micro:bit
in Python**
— 157 —

Remote Control Car
— 162 —

Programming NeoPixels
— 173 —

Refrigerator Data
— 181 —

Bottle Rocket
— 188 —

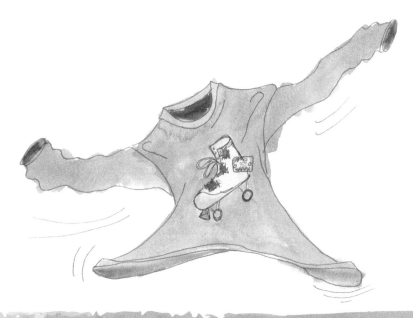

Wearable Computing

Combining the micro:bit with conductive thread and LEDs makes it possible to create wearable circuitry. Using these soft circuits, you can sew LEDs, buzzers, and sensors on clothes, bags, and other fabric. Adding the micro:bit makes these circuits programmable and even interactive. You can make and program "smart" clothes!

There is a lot of room for creativity in this project. You may incorporate soft circuits into any design you wish.

To make the project truly wearable, you will need a way to power the micro:bit so you don't have to be connected to the computer. Use the standard micro:bit battery box, a power bank, or a micro:bit add-on battery board or case.

Caution: Do not get the micro:bit or other circuitry wet. So, you will not be able to wash garments that include such circuitry.

Materials
micro:bit, 1 USB cable & battery pack, a set of Adafruit LED sequins or LEDs, conductive thread, normal thread, 1 piece of felt, sewing needle, scissor, paper, alligator clips, 2 bare clips (alligator clips without cables), 2 sewable metal snaps.

Make

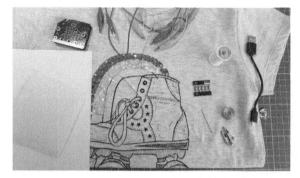

1. Organize the materials.

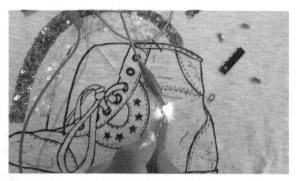

2. Test each of the LEDs to check their color and which legs are positive and negative.

3. Position the LEDs and micro:bit where you wish them to appear in your design.

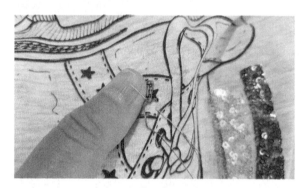

4. Align the LED lights so the plus and minus sides are in rows.

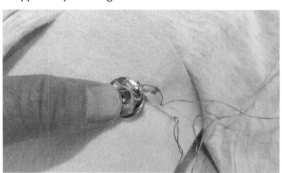

5. On the back of the fabric underneath the LEDs, attach a small piece of extra fabric or felt. This extra fabric will help keep the circuit flat and provide a place to attach conductive thread. You will add two snaps to this fabric (you only need one side of the snap each). One snap will be the hub for all the negative LED connections, the other snap will be the hub for all the positive LED connections. They do not snap together and should not touch.

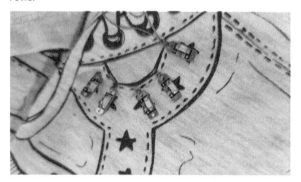

6. Use the conductive thread to sew tightly through all the negative LED connections. Loop the thread through the holes several times. Connect this thread to one snap. This snap is now the hub for the negative LED connections.

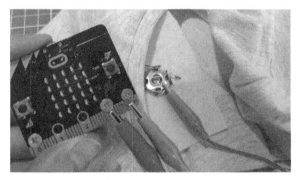

7. Connect an alligator clip from the negative snap hub and to GND on the micro:bit.

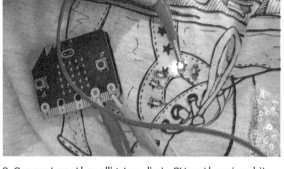

8. Connect another alligator clip to 3V on the micro:bit. Touch the other end of this clip to the positive connections of the LEDs to see if the circuit is working.

9. Next, use a different piece of conductive thread to sew all the positive connections of the LEDs together and connect them all to another snap hub under the fabric.

10. On the fabric inside your shirt, you should have two snaps. One snap is the positive hub connected to all the positive sides of the LEDs. The other snap is the negative (ground/GND) hub. Do not sew the positive and negative sides together. The conductive thread connected to one snap may not touch the threads connected to the other snap.

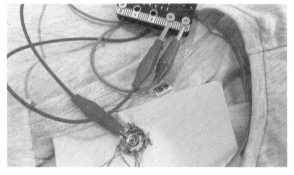

11. Use alligator clips to test the LEDs by connecting the positive snap hub to the 3V and the negative snap hub to the GND of the micro:bit.

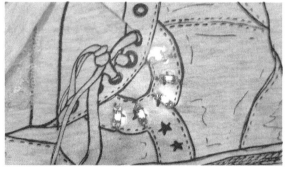

12. If you connected them correctly, all the LEDs will light up.

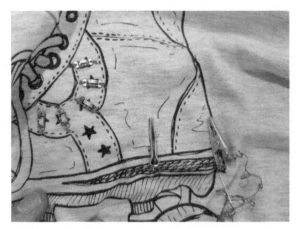

13. Sew two bare clips to your shirt with conductive thread. These clips will hold the micro:bit in place, but also allow you to remove it as needed. One clip will connect to the GND hole in the micro:bit. Use conductive thread to connect this clip through the shirt to the negative snap hub underneath the shirt.

The other clip connects to one of the pins of the micro:bit. Use conductive thread to connect this clip through the shirt to the positive snap hub underneath. Do not cross these conductive threads.

14. Program the micro:bit and connect the micro:bit to your project with the clips. In this build, the positive clip is connected to pin P1, so all the programming uses the `write to pin P1` blocks. You can even sew the micro:bit to your shirt (with normal thread), but if you do that, you cannot wash this shirt!

Tutorial movie

There is a tutorial movie about how to make this wearable project. Go to the website microbit.inventtolearn.com to watch it.

Connections

Look carefully at the schematic drawing below to see how the LEDs should be connected to the micro:bit. All the connections should be sewn using conductive thread on the underside of the fabric.

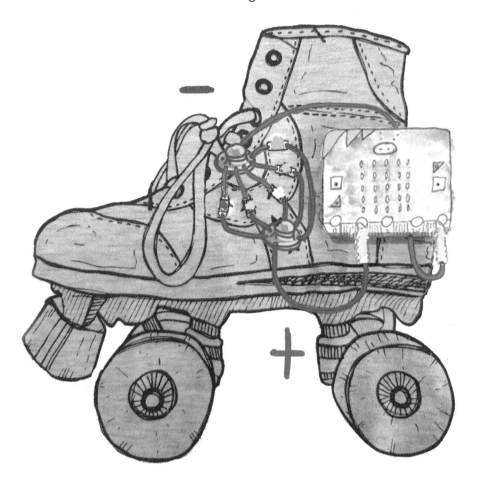

Test each LED before sewing them to the fabric.

Test the circuit using alligator clips before sewing the LEDs with conductive thread.

The snaps are just being used as a convenient hub connection for the conductive thread. They do not snap together. Mark next to each snap hub which is positive and which is negative.

All negative leads of the LEDs are sewn to a half a snap. This negative snap hub will then connect to GND on the micro:bit.

The positive leads of the LEDs are all sewn to the other half of a snap. This positive snap hub is connected to P1 on the micro:bit.

Do not cross or connect the positive side of your circuit to the negative side. Do not sew the conductive thread across the LEDs from the positive side to the negative side.

The snap hubs are connected to bare clips, which also hold the micro:bit in place. This allows you to easily remove the micro:bit from this project.

If you do not need to remove the micro:bit, you do not need to use the clips. Directly sew the conductive thread from each hub through the P1 and GND holes. Loop the conductive thread tightly through the micro:bit holes many times and tie tightly.

When you are done and everything is working, you might want to cover the thread and snaps with tape. This will ensure that your snaps or thread do not cross or touch when the fabric is moved or worn.

Ways to power your wearable project

For this project, the lightest power supply will make your wearable even more wearable. The photos in this project show a powerboard that connects to the back of a micro:bit which uses a lightweight coin cell battery for power. There are lots of these available from different companies. If you don't have a powerboard, you can make a pocket for your battery, or feed the cables through the fabric and attach the battery pack out of view.

LEDs and power

The Adafruit LEDs shown in the build photos are very power efficient and can be powered with a small battery pack or coin cell battery pack. If you add too many LEDs, or your batteries are running out, you will see them go dim. If you use regular LEDs, especially larger ones, you may see the LEDS go dim even faster.

Programming

The simple code for this project is just a place to start.

Pressing the buttons cause your LEDs to turn on an off at different intervals. Jumping causes a dancing animation and flashing lights.

- Create the program on the following page
- Find the `on 3g` block as one of the options in the `on shake` block
- Name your file
- Download the program to your micro:bit
- Test your wearable creation
- Debug the program if necessary

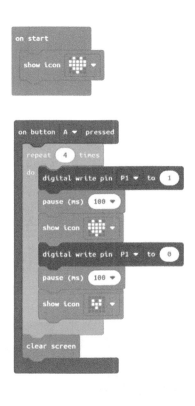

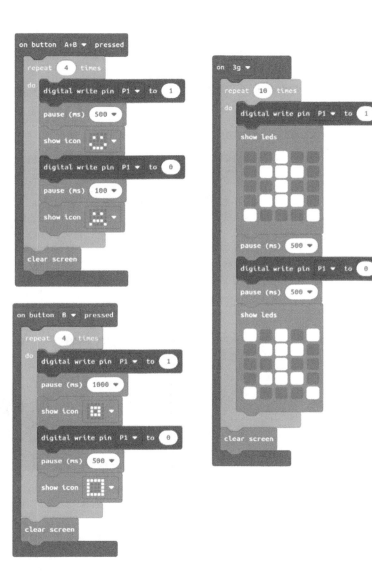

Understanding the code

When the A, B, or both buttons are pressed, animate an icon on the micro:bit display and flash the LED attached to P1 four times.

The `on 3g` block runs when 3gs of force are generated by jumping. It flashes the LEDs attached to P1 and plays a jumping animation on the micro:bit.

Challenges

- Make a second (or third) circuit of LED lights by using more snaps and connections. Program those lights to behave differently.
- Program your wearable invention to react to the light level in a room. Turn the lights on (or make them perform) when it gets dark.

Inspiration for wearable projects!

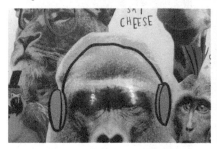

A shirt with LEDs and a coin cell battery.

Frida Kahlo with LEDs

An LED badge

Light up mask

A smiley face badge

A skirt with LEDs that light up when you dance

A tie and shoes with LED strips.

A bag with LEDs that turn on when it gets dark

A jacket with LEDs that light when you move

Talking micro:bit in Python

Making the micro:bit talk would be really cool! MakeCode does not currently support text-to-speech, so we will use a different programming language called Python.

Python is a popular text-based language that uses words as computer instructions rather than blocks like MakeCode or Scratch, but don't be scared. This project will teach you what you need to learn in order to make a micro:bit talk. We will use MicroPython for this project.

Although MakeCode has a Python editor, it has limited functionality and doesn't currently include text-to-speech capabilities. So, we will use MicroPython for this project.

Materials
micro:bit, USB cable & battery pack, 2 alligator clips, powered speaker, wire stripper.

Make

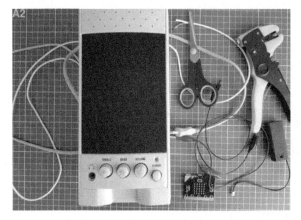

1. Gather all of your tools and materials

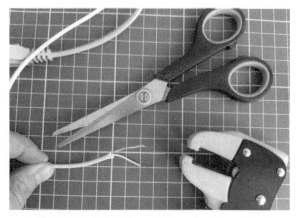

2. Connect the speaker wires to P0 and GND. If there is not enough exposed wire to make a good connection, use a wire stripper. If your speaker has a headphone jack, don't wreck your speakers if you need them for other things!

Tips

- We recommend a powered speaker for this project because of its amplification.
- If you have a micro:bit V2, this will work without a speaker.

Connections

The speaker must be connected to pin P0 and GND.

If you hacked an old computer speaker, the plus wire must go to pin P0 and the minus wire must go to GND.

You may of course also use headphones and connect them as you did in the *Jingle Bells* project.

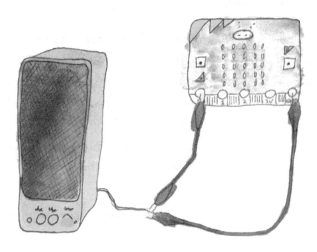

Programming

Go to the MicroPython website python.microbit.org.

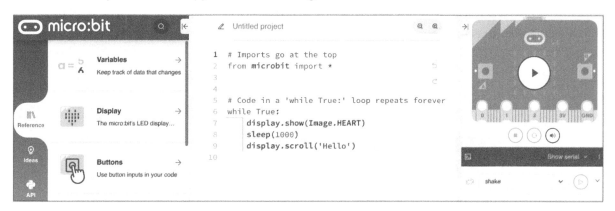

The following code needs to be typed in to the editor. You might notice that some of the instructions perform the same function as blocks in MakeCode. Be precise with spelling and capitalization, MicroPython doesn't like typos.

```python
# Imports go at the top
from microbit import *
import music
import speech

# Code in a 'while True:' loop repeats forever
while True:
    display.show(Image.HEART)
    sleep(1000)
    display.scroll('Hello')
    music.play (music.PYTHON)
    sleep (1000)
    display.show(Image.HAPPY)
    sleep(400)
    speech.say ('Learn to Invent,')
    speech.say ('With the microbit!')
    sleep (1000)
```

Send the code to the micro:bit

When you are done writing your code, the next step is to send the code to the micro:bit.

Connect the micro:bit to your computer. Then click the three dots to the right of the **Send to micro:bit** button and select **Connect**. Follow the onscreen instructions to connect to your micro:bit.

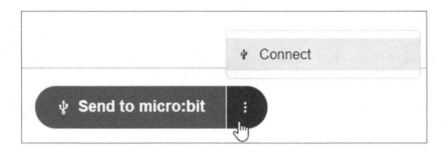

"Flash" is another term MicroPython uses for sending code to the micro:bit.

The program will run on the micro:bit. Debug if necessary. Error messages will be displayed below the code or on the micro:bit.

For help, click the **Reference** tab on the left side panel.

Understanding the code

MicroPython needs special libraries to add music and speech to the list of things the micro:bit can do.

- **import music** enables playing music on the micro:bit
- **import speech** enables text to speech

while True: is like a forever loop, the instructions underneath run until the program is stopped.

display.scroll scrolls the text in between the single quote marks on the micro:bit.

display.show displays an icon on the micro:bit. In some browsers, as you type **display.show** a menu will pop up with suggestions. If you don't see this list, just type **Image.HEART** as shown. To find other icons, check the MicroPython tutorial site.

sleep is the same as pause in MakeCode.

music.play plays a bit of music. In some browsers, when you type **music.play**, a pop-up menu appears from which you can choose the music file you wish to play. If you don't see a pop-up list, the list of available music can be found on the MicroPython tutorial site.

speech.say causes the text in quotes to be spoken through the speaker connected to the micro:bit

Be careful to use capital letters, periods, quotation marks, and apostrophes in your program exactly as shown. For example, Sleep is not the same as sleep.

Remember to send the code to the micro:bit every time you change your code.

Help the micro:bit speak better

With a bit of extra code, you can play around with the pitch, speed, throat, and mouth of the voice in your speech.

pitch – How high or low the voice sounds (0=high and 255=low)

speed – How quickly it speaks (0=impossibly fast and 255=sleepy)

mouth – How tight-lipped the voice is (0=very tight and 255=loose)

throat – How relaxed is the voice (0=tense and 255=relaxed)

See how these parameters are used in the program below.

- Change your code under **while True**: to:
  speech.say('I am a microbit', speed=90, pitch=60, throat=190, mouth=190)
- You can copy and paste this line of code and play around with the speed, pitch, throat, and mouth

```
1   # Imports go at the top
2   from microbit import *
3   import speech
4
5   # Code in a 'while True:' loop repeats forever
6   while True:
7       display.show(Image.CONFUSED)
8       sleep(1000)
9       display.scroll('microbit')
10      sleep (500)
11      speech.say('I am a microbit', speed=90, pitch=60, throat=190, mouth=190)
12      sleep (1000)
13      speech.say('I am a robot', speed=50, pitch=100, throat=110, mouth=160)
14      sleep (1000)
15      speech.say('I am a computer', speed=80, pitch=200, throat=200, mouth=50)
16      sleep (1000)
17
```

Tips

- The **Reference** tab on the left side of the screen not only has explanations of code, but also has pre-made snippets of code you can drag and drop onto the program work area.
- If you make errors, they will be displayed on the screen. Read those messages carefully. They will tell you which line number is a problem and what kind of error you made. This helps you find errors and debug your Python program.

Challenges

- Explore the tutorials on the MicroPython website.
- What are some cool features in MicroPython that you haven't found in MakeCode?
- Can you make the micro:bit sing?

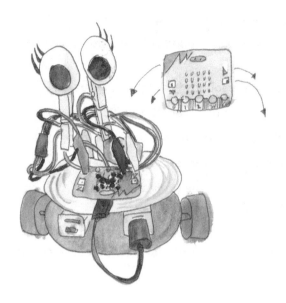

Remote Control Car

Let's make a robot car using recycled materials like cardboard, discarded CDs, broken toys, or wood!

This project is a bit tricky since it uses three micro:bits—two to control motors driving independent wheels and one as a remote control. Each of the micro:bits runs its own MakeCode program.

Since servo motors need a lot of power, this project works best if a rechargeable USB power bank is used.

It may be possible to use only two micro:bits if you use an add-on motor board to control the motors.

Materials
3 micro:bits, 2 USB cables, 1 micro:bit battery pack, 2 rechargeable USB power banks, 2 continuous (360) servos, 6 alligator clip to male pin leads, a CD, 2 wheels (made from cardboard, wood, soda bottle tops, or from an old car toy), 1 ping pong ball (or cork), 2 clothespins, googly eyes, hot glue gun, adhesive Velcro strips, scissors, cardboard, tape.

Make

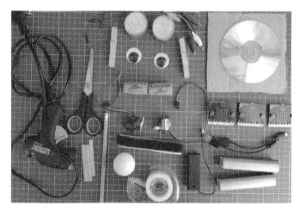

1. Gather all your materials.

2. Glue the wheels on the 360 servo shafts. They need to dry completely before you use them.

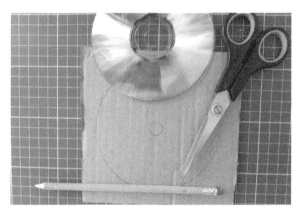

3. Draw and cut a circle out of cardboard. Poke a hole through the middle to push through cables.

4. Attach the two power banks to the cardboard with Velcro. Put two more strips of Velcro on the top of the power banks.

Be sure to have the power banks facing in opposite directions so that they will easily connect to a micro:bit on each side of the car.

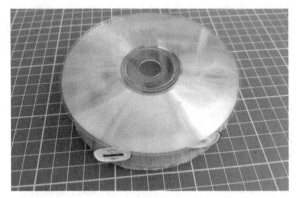

5. Adhere the CD to the top of the power banks with Velcro fasteners. The base for the micro:bits does not have to be a CD, but CDs are usually easy to find, and are the right size, lightweight, and rigid.

6. Attach the two micro:bits to the top of the CD with Velcro. Make sure that the pins are close to the center hole where the cables will pass through.

7. Glue the servos (with a lot of glue) to the bottom of the cardboard circle. Wait at least 5 minutes until the wheels are sturdy and fixed to the car.

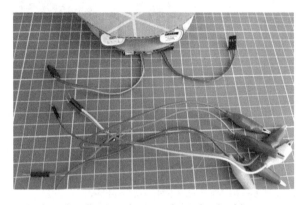

8. Gather the alligator clip to male pin lead cables.

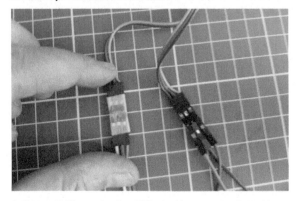

9. Connect the male pin cables to the servo motors. Use some tape to make sure they don't come apart.

10. Pull all the cables through the hole of the CD.

11. Cut a ping pong ball in half and glue each half on the bottom of the car. You also can use other materials, such as two corks. This helps steady the car.

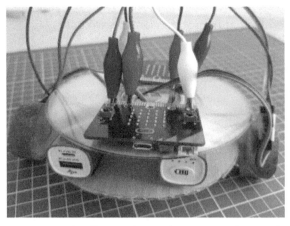

12. Connect the alligator clips to the two micro:bits. Look carefully at the connection diagram on the next page.

13. Download the code to each of the micro:bits and test the car. Once working, disconnect from your computer and connect each micro:bit to a powerbank. The two micro:bits control the servos. Their code is slightly different because they are positioned on opposite sides of your car. You will use a third micro:bit as a remote control.

14. If you're feeling creative, give your car a funny face with clothespins and googly eyes.

Video tutorial

There is a video online showing how the car is assembled at microbit.inventtolearn.com

2020-08-06 13.47.24.mp4

Connections

Look carefully at the diagram to see how everything is connected.

You have already connected continuous servos to the micro:bit in earlier projects. The dark cable from the servo goes to the GND, the red to 3V and the lightest colored cable goes to P0. The two micro:bits are positioned so the connections are near the center hole of the CD, so each USB power bank can easily be connected to the micro:bit.

Programming - Remote control

Let's start with the code for the remote control.

- Create the following code.
- Read it. See if you can predict what it will do.
- Test it in the Simulator.
- Save the project with a filename like *RC Car*.
- Download the code to the micro:bit
- Tilt the micro:bit and press both buttons to see what happens.

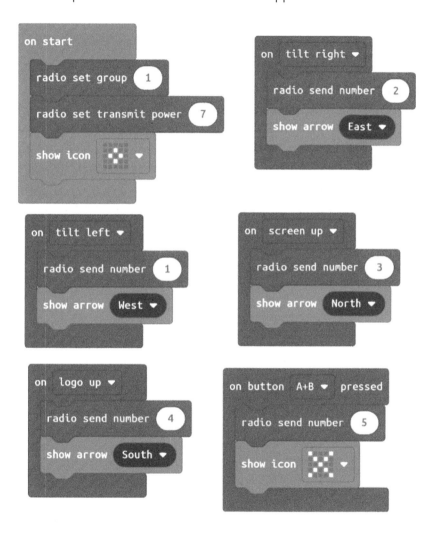

Understanding the code - Remote control

The `on start` block selects the channel for the radio communication. You are free to change this number, especially if you are in a room with lots of other micro:bits communicating via radio. Just make sure you use the same radio group number for your remote control and the car code.

The `radio set transmit power` block is set to maximum broadcast strength of 7.

When you tilt the micro:bit in various directions, its display should change and a number is broadcast via radio. That number will signal what the wheels should do.

Note: The `show arrow` North, South, East, and West blocks do not actually display arrows that point in accurate compass directions, even though the micro:bit does have a compass sensor. These are just convenient up, down, right, and left arrow icons to use. You could draw your own arrow icons if you want.

Programming - Car servos

Your car contains two more micro:bits, each one attached to a continuous servo capable of turning 360 degrees. Each of the micro:bits has their own slightly different code because they are on opposite sides of the car. We will call the micro:bits on the top of your car X and Y since the vehicle is round and the micro:bits are mounted on opposite sides. It doesn't make sense to name them left/right or front/back since that will change as the car moves.

Remember to add the servo blocks from the **Extensions** menu and use the continuous servo blocks.

Create the code for micro:bit X

- Create the following code.
- Save the project with a filename like *Motor X*.
- Download the code to one of the micro:bits on the top of your car.
- Grab the micro:bit with the remote control code on it and see if it is controlling the motor attached to micro:bit X.

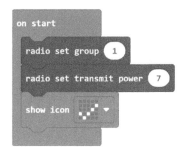

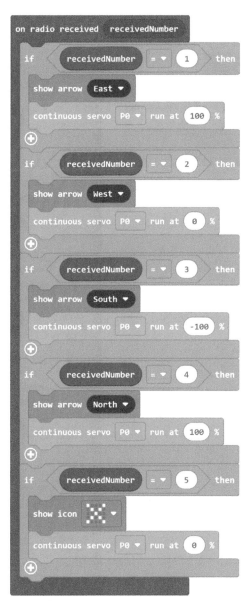

Create the code for micro:bit Y

- Disconnect the first micro:bit from the computer.
- Create the following code.
- Save the project with a filename like *Motor Y*.
- Connect the other micro:bit to your computer.
- Download the code to this micro:bit
- Try the remote control micro:bit and see if it is controlling the motor attached to micro:bit Y.

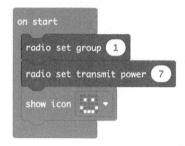

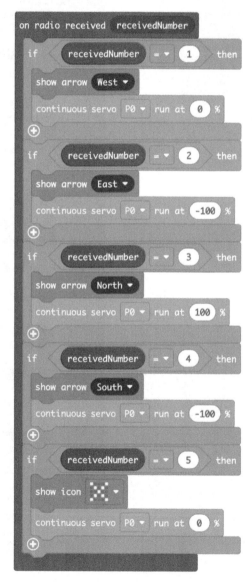

Understanding the code - Car servos

Both sets of code are quite similar.

`on start` sets the radio channel, sets maximum radio power, and displays an icon to indicate that your program is working. Make sure to set the same radio group channel used in the remote control code.

The `on radio received` block listens for a number to be broadcast by a nearby micro:bit. When it "hears" a number, it swings into action. It sets the value of the variable `receivedNumber` to the number it hears.

The `if/then` blocks check the numerical value received and either turn the attached servo in a particular direction or tell the servo to stop spinning. Arrow icons indicating direction appear on the micro:bit display.

With these two similar sets of code on the different micro:bits, the servos should work independently when you drive the car with your micro:bit remote control.

You may have to swap the code on the two servos in order to get the arrows to point in the proper direction. Play with the power level of the servos to make your vehicle move faster or slower.

Understanding continuous servos

Continuous servos can rotate 360 degrees. This makes them better wheels than 180 degree servos.

Change the number in the `continuous servo run at` block from –100% to 100%.

- 100% will make it spin as fast as it can one way.
- -100% will spin as fast as it can in the opposite direction.
- 0% will stop it.
- Use numbers smaller than 100 to make it spin slower.

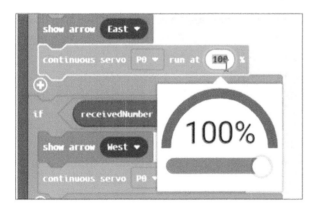

When one servo spins and the other doesn't, the vehicle should turn (Received number 1, 2).

When both servos are turning at similar rates in the same direction, your vehicle should go forward or backward (Received number 3, 4).

When both servos are set to 0%, the car should stop (Received number 5).

micro:bit X		micro:bit Y	
Received number	Motor %	Received number	Motor %
1	100 %	1	0 %
2	0 %	2	-100 %
3	-100 %	3	100 %
4	100 %	4	-100 %
5	0 %	5	0 %

Because the motors are mounted on opposite sides of the car, forward and backward motor settings are reversed. You will need to test your car to find out which way each motor turns for different servo settings.

Challenges

- Can you change the code to make your car speed up and slow down?
- Headlights or directional signals might be cool additions to your remote-control car.
- Invent bumpers to cause the car to backup when it collides with something.
- Give your car a horn.
- Try making the car with a micro:bit motor board. Then you only need two micro:bits in the project instead of three.
- Can you change the code to make it more compact?
- Can your control two cars with one micro:bit remote control?

Motor boards

This project is a good candidate for using a micro:bit motor board. These boards simplify using motors with a micro:bit. They often include extra batteries that power multiple motors and support special connectors. Some have extensions to make programming simpler. Find recommended motor boards in the *Further Adventures* section of the *Resources*.

Programming NeoPixels

NeoPixels are tiny, programmable, color-changing LEDs manufactured by Adafruit Industries (adafruit.com). They are especially popular in wearable projects and as indicator lights. NeoPixels make cool additions to micro:bit projects since they require little power, can be addressed individually or in groups, and can change color. Some micro:bit expansion boards feature built-in NeoPixels.

Best of all, there are NeoPixels extension blocks available for MakeCode. This project will help you understand NeoPixel programming in MakeCode and should work with any NeoPixel hardware.

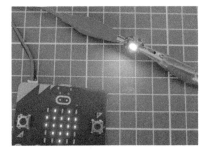

Sewable NeoPixel

NeoPixel Strip

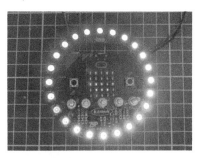

NeoPixel Ring or Zip HALO

NeoPixel ZIP

Servo:Lite motor board

bit:booster

Connecting the NeoPixels to the micro:bit

Unless the NeoPixels are integrated into a board like the bit:booster, you will need to connect three wires to: 3V, GND, and either P0, P1, or P2.

The NeoPixel strips with alligator clips from Adafruit are super easy to connect to micro:bit pins because there are alligator clips already attached. Otherwise, you can figure out how to connect three wires to the micro:bit.

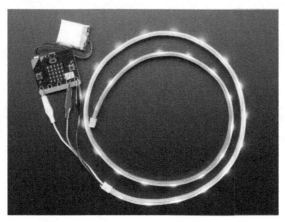

Adding the NeoPixel extension into MakeCode

- Click **Extensions** on the MakeCode Toolbox.
- Type Neopixel or click on the Lights and Display button under the search field. Click on the NeoPixel extension.

There should now be a new set of NeoPixel blocks in the MakeCode Toolbox. These blocks will save with your project, but you will need to add them again for other projects.

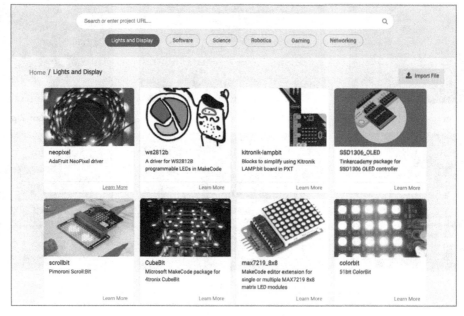

Programming the NeoPixels

Once the NeoPixel extension is installed, you may begin programming with blocks specifically designed to control these LEDs. The first thing you need to do is tell MakeCode about your attached NeoPixel. This is called initializing the environment (setting it up).

- Count the number of LEDs in your NeoPixel gizmo.
- Create an `on start` block.
- Insert a `set strip to NeoPixel at pin...` block.
- Change the pin dropdown to indicate which micro:bit pin you connected the NeoPixels to.
- Change the number in the `with ___ leds` field to the number of LEDs in your NeoPixels.
- Leave the `RGB format` dropdown as it is unless you are using a NeoPixel that contains white LEDs.

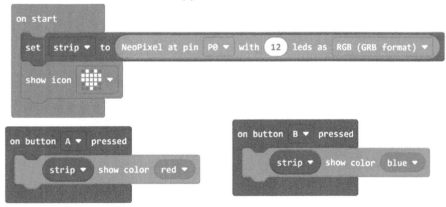

Now, MakeCode will initialize the NeoPixel device whenever the program runs.

Note: If you connect more than one NeoPixel, MakeCode will automatically generate `set strip` blocks like the one above, but will name them `strip2` , `strip3` , etc... You also have the ability to rename the strips.

Add some button control
- Create the following program, predict what it will do, and download it to the micro:bit.
- Press the A or B button and see what happens.

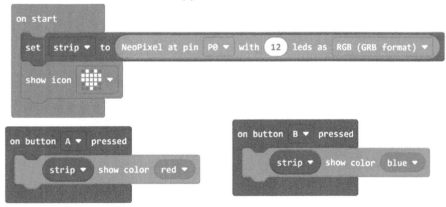

You can make a rainbow
`strip show rainbow from 1 to 360` lights each pixel with a different color of the rainbow.

Try this program

Remember to specify how many LEDs are in your NeoPixel device.

- What does the program do?
- What happens if you shift pixels by another number?
- Try to shift pixels by -1. What happens?

When you ask the NeoPixels to do something specific, like shift, rotate, or light a range of LEDs, you may need to add a `strip show` block to force the NeoPixels to update and make the changes visible.

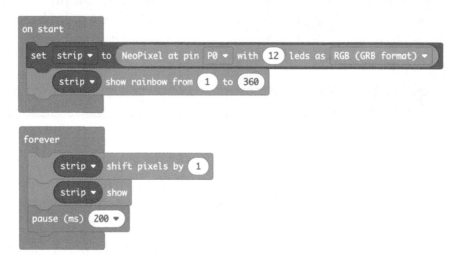

A slight variation to try

- How is rotating pixels different from shifting them?
- Try different values for rotating pixels. What happens?
- Try rotating pixels by half of the number of pixels you have. What happens?
- What happens if you reduce the number 360 in the `show rainbow from 1 to 360` block in `on start`?

Be specific

The NeoPixel blocks can control specific pixels. The pixels are numbered starting at zero. Use the
set pixel color at block (found in the **...more** section of the **NeoPixel** panel in the Toolbox) to specify the
color of a specific pixel. Remember to use the strip show block to display the changes.

```
on start
    set strip ▼ to NeoPixel at pin P0 ▼ with 12 leds as RGB (GRB format) ▼
        strip ▼ show color red ▼
```

```
on button A ▼ pressed
    strip ▼ set pixel color at 5 to yellow ▼
    strip ▼ show
```

So random

Make the following modification to the program above.

- After you insert the pick random variable, use the range 0 to the number of pixels – 1.
- Download the program to the micro:bit.
- Press button A repeatedly.

```
on start
    set strip ▼ to NeoPixel at pin P0 ▼ with 12 leds as RGB (GRB format) ▼
        strip ▼ show color red ▼
```

```
on button A ▼ pressed
    strip ▼ set pixel color at pick random 0 to 11 to yellow ▼
    strip ▼ show
```

Ho! Ho! Ho!

Imagine a 12-light NeoPixel ring. The following program turns it into a push button wreath.

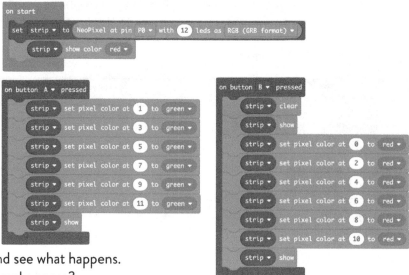

- Press A or B and see what happens.
- Does the code make sense?

Within range

In this program, we define a range or region of LEDs in the NeoPixel as a variable in order to change that entire range at once.

We will use the `set range` block from the **NeoPixel** blocks in the Toolbox. However, we want to set two different ranges of LEDs. So, for the second `set range` block, we will select the `set range` block a second time from the **NeoPixel** block panel and MakeCode will add a new `set range2` block to the workspace. Do it again to get `set range3`, etc... In other words, each time you request a `set range` block, MakeCode automatically creates a new variable.

`set range` takes two inputs—the LED position where you wish to begin and how many LEDs should be included in that range. For example, if you have a 12 LED NeoPixel that you wish to divide into two sections, you might try a program like this.

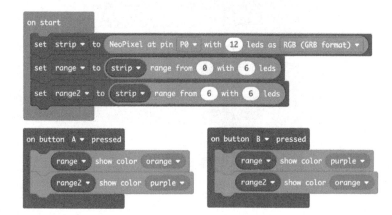

Choose your own pixel colors

NeoPixels can be set to a larger range of colors than the ten options built into MakeCode (red, orange, yellow, green...) Turn a pixel the exact color you wish using the RGB system. RGB is short for Red, Green, and Blue. It is one of the most common ways of specifying colors in computer displays and TVs.

Let's make new colors!

Add the following code to your project. Make sure to include an `on start` block that sets the number of pixels in your NeoPixel and specifies the pin the pixels are connected to.

- Try it out in the Simulator
- Download it to the micro:bit

```
on button A+B ▼ pressed
    strip ▼ set pixel color at ( pick random 0 to 11 ) to  red 0 green 255 blue 255
    strip ▼ show
```

Understanding the code

The selections in the NeoPixel blocks include green and blue, but what if you want something in between, like aqua?

Aqua is a mixture of the following red, green, and blue values. Red = 0, Green = 255, and Blue = 255.

When A+B are pressed, a random pixel will turn aqua.

For more colors, change the RGB values to any number from 0 to 255. RGB color values can be found online at sites like rapidtables.com/web/color/RGB_Color.html. You will see the numbers to fill in for Red, Green and Blue for any color you like.

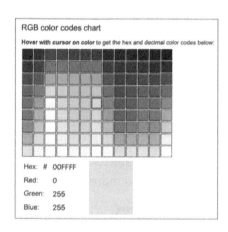

Try this!

What happens if you replace one of the RGB values with a random number? Add the following blocks and experiment.

```
on shake ▼
    strip ▼ show color  black ▼
    repeat 100 times
    do
        strip ▼ set pixel color at ( pick random 0 to 11 ) to  red ( pick random 0 to 255 ) green 70 blue 70
        strip ▼ show
        pause (ms) 100 ▼
```

Do the twist

In this program, we use the acceleration value (found in the **Input** panel) to send the pixels in one direction or the opposite when the micro:bit is tilted left or right.

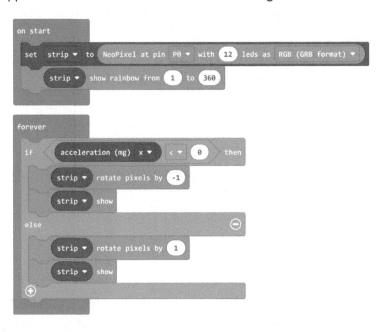

Create the program above

- Download it to the micro:bit
- Tilt the micro:bit left or right

Any micro:bit sensor value can be used to control NeoPixels in many different ways. The colors and patterns can be more than just decoration, they can represent what's happening in the physical world.

Challenges

- Use different sensors to control the light patterns.
- Can you create numerical light patterns, like odd and even numbers or multiples?
- What can you decorate with NeoPixels?
- Be sure to share your MakeCode projects online so others can learn from them!

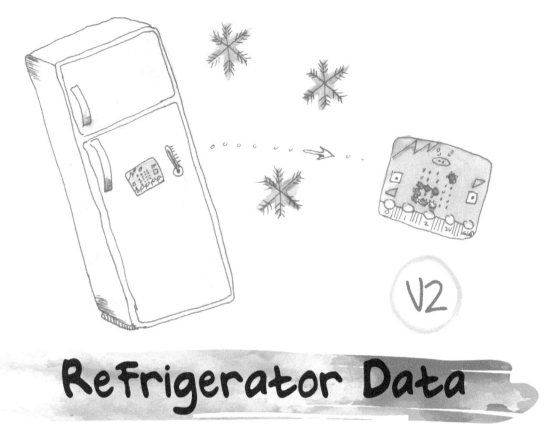

Refrigerator Data

In this project you will learn about data analysis on the micro:bit. We know the micro:bit can show the temperature like in the project *What's the Temperature*. Now we will take it one step further and program the micro:bit to record temperature changes over time. You will put a micro:bit in the refrigerator to collect data. After a while, you can take it out and look at the data to observe how the temperature dropped. For this project you don't have to build anything, just put the code on the micro:bit and attach the battery pack and put it in your refrigerator. In the second part of this project, we will use the radio function and a second micro:bit to record the temperature data in real time.

Note: Data logging only works with the micro:bit V2.

Materials
1 micro:bit V2, 1 battery pack, USB cable.

Add datalogger extension

To collect data using the micro:bit add the **Data Logger** blocks to MakeCode. Open the **Extensions** and search for *datalogger*. Once you add this extension you will see the **Data Logger** blocks in MakeCode.

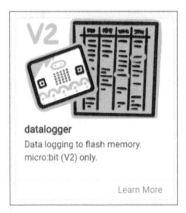

Program - Simple datalogger

The Data Logger blocks give the micro:bit V2 the ability to collect and save data from the sensors over a period of time. This is called "logging" the data. The data is saved internally in the micro:bit until you are ready to use it.

- Create the following program in MakeCode
- Make a variable **start**
- The `every 200 ms` block is in the **Loop** section of the Toolbox
- The `log data` block is in the **Data Logger** section of the Toolbox
- Name and save your code
- In the `log data` block, define the name of the data and the source of the data to collect. Give the column a name, in this case, "temp" (short for "temperature") and drag in a `temperature` block to replace the default value.

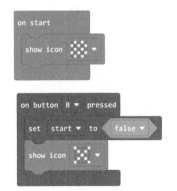
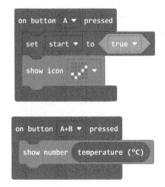
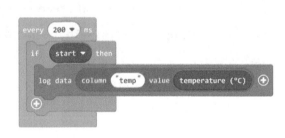

Understanding the code – Simple datalogger

The data collected by the `log data` block is organized into columns, along with the time of collection. In this project, we are only collecting one column of data, the temperature. If you want to collect more data from other micro:bit sensors, click on the + sign in the `log data` block.

In this program, the **start** variable controls when to start or stop logging data. Button A is the start button, and pressing it sets the **start** variable to true. Button B is the stop button, and pressing it sets **start** to false. Pressing A and B together just shows the current temperature.

The `every 200 ms` loop checks the **start** variable to see if the datalogger should run. If the variable is true, it runs the `log data` block, collecting and saving the current temperature. It then waits 200 milliseconds and runs again.

Loops run in the background, allowing other code to continue executing.

The 200 milliseconds in the `every 200 ms` loop is an arbitrary amount of time. The loop could run faster or slower. A higher wait time means it will run slower, and you will collect less data. A lower wait time means it will run faster, and you will collect more data.

Different projects might require longer or shorter times. You can balance having too much or too little data by adjusting how often you log the data.

Test the program using the Simulator

- Click the A button in the Simulator to start measuring
- A **Show data Simulator** button will appear. Press the button to see the growing data collection displayed.
- "Change" the temperature with your mouse
- Press the **Go back** button to exit the simulation
- Remember, this isn't real sensor data—just a simulation

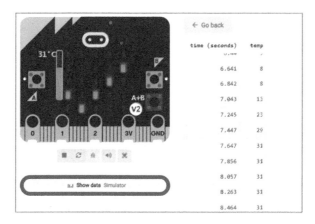

Recording real temperatures

After testing the code in the Simulator, download it to the micro:bit. Follow these steps to collect 10 minutes of temperature data from inside the refrigerator.

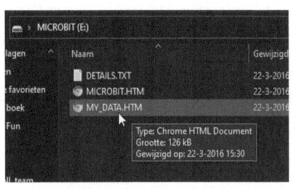

1. Connect a battery pack to the micro:bit. Put it in the refrigerator and press A. The micro:bit will start measuring the temperature. Close the door. After ten minutes, remove the micro:bit from the refrigerator and press B to stop collecting temperature data.

2. Connect the micro:bit to your computer and go to the micro:bit in the File Explorer (Windows) or Finder (Mac). You will see there is an extra file on your micro:bit. MY_DATA.HTM. Double click on this file to open it.

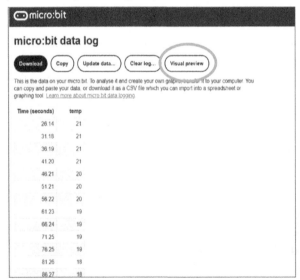

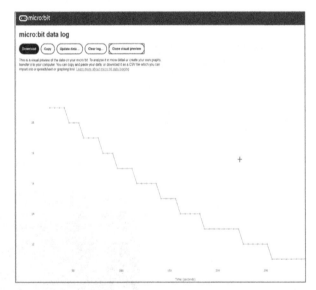

3. When the file opens, click on Visual preview. This will open in your default browser. It uses a bit of clever behind-the-scenes programming to display the data and other options for saving or copying the data.

4. Observe how quickly the temperature dropped over time. The Y-axis shows the recorded temperature and the X-axis represents elapsed time in seconds.

Challenges

- What happens if you change the collection rate of 200 ms to 1 minute? How will the graph change?
- What other data can you analyze with the micro:bit?

Transmitting remote data in real time

In some projects, it may be inconvenient to collect the data on a micro:bit and wait to see the results. You may expect to collect a lot of data that makes the file too big. If you collect too much data, the micro:bit might misbehave or lose the information. You might want to see the data in real time, like a speedometer or thermometer.

For this project, you will need a second micro:bit. We use the radio function to send data from one micro:bit to another in real time. One micro:bit will be inside the refrigerator broadcasting temperature sensor data. The second micro:bit receives and collects the data. This receiving micro:bit is outside the refrigerator, connected to a computer. That allows you to use the data logging tools to see real-time changes in temperature or save the data for further investigation. For this project to work, the sending and receiving micro:bits must be within 70 meters of each other. Closer is better.

Program - The sending micro:bit

One micro:bit will broadcast data from a remote location. This code is almost the same as the code from the previous simple datalogger project. The difference is that the micro:bit inside the refrigerator will not save the data, it will transmit data to a second micro:bit every 1,000 ms.

- Create a variable, **start**.
- Set the transmission power to its maximum, 7. This block is in the **... more** section of the **Radio** panel.
- Both micro:bits need to be set to the same radio group. In this case, radio group 1.
- Recreate the following code.
- Download the program to the sending/broadcasting micro:bit that will go into the fridge.

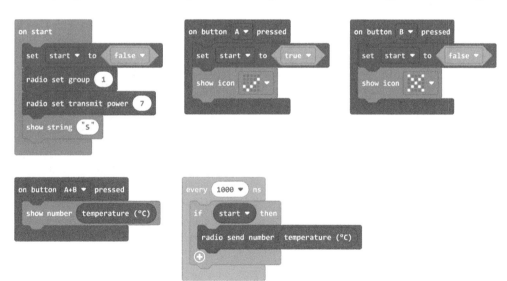

Program - The data receiving micro:bit

Download the following code to the receiving micro:bit. It collects the data received from the sending micro:bit in real time. This micro:bit stays connected to the computer.

- Add the datalogging blocks from **Extensions**.
- Create the following code.
- Choose the time format you desire, from milliseconds to days, with the `timestamp` block.
- The `mirror data to serial` block controls whether the data is sent to the serial port on the connected computer. If you want to see the data in real time, it should be on. If you choose not to mirror the data to the serial port, it will only be logged in the internal micro:bit memory for later use.
- Download the program to the data-receiving micro:bit.

Once the code is on both micro:bits, put the sender in the fridge and keep the receiver connected to your computer.

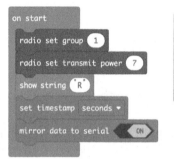

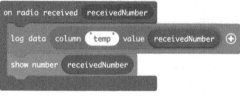

1. Connect a battery pack to the sending micro:bit. Put it in the refrigerator and press A. This sends data to the other micro:bit every second (1,000 ms). Close the door.

2. Attach the receiving micro:bit to the computer. You should see the incoming data displayed on the receiving micro:bit.

The MakeCode console will also display the incoming data.

When you are done with the experiment, take the sender micro:bit out of the fridge and press B.

Display your data

When the micro:bit is connected to the computer you can see the data it is collecting in real time. Click the **Show data Device** button to see a table and graph of the data. You can even download this data in comma separated value format (CSV) with the download button on the right. Open the file in any spreadsheet software. Warning: At the time of publication, if you set the timestamp to any value (except none), MakeCode draws both time and the sensor data on the same graph, which makes the temperature change hard to see. However, you can download good data to use in any spreadsheet program to create a graph of temperature fluctuations over time. To see just the temperature data in real time in MakeCode, like below, set the `set timestamp` to **none**.

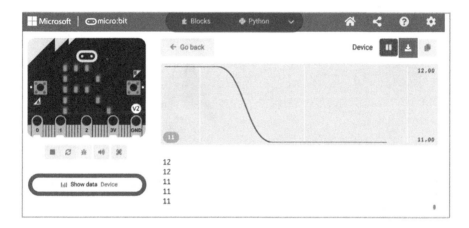

Tips

- Make sure that your sender and receiver micro:bit are not too far apart. The thick refrigerator door may make it more difficult to share data.
- Remember, the micro:bit is a tiny, inexpensive computer. It is not a precise scientific instrument. Occasionally, you may see fluctuations in timing or inaccurate sensor data.
- If it is not convenient to connect the receiving micro:bit to a computer, the micro:bit can save the data in a file on the micro:bit for analysis later. If it is connected to a computer, it will transmit the data and no file will be saved. If it is not connected to a computer, it will save the file. However, you can force the data to be saved locally on the micro:bit by switching the `mirror data to serial port` block to OFF.

Challenges

- What else can you measure around the classroom or in your house?
- Can you measure the speed of a toy train or car?
- Create a wall sign that reports the temperature outside and tells classmates whether to wear a jacket at recess.

Bottle Rocket

Imagine you are a rocket scientist designing a rocket out of a recycled drink bottle. The goal is to launch it as high as possible. By attaching a micro:bit you will be able to measure the time in seconds between liftoff and the peak of its flight. Of course, you may experiment with different rocket designs and forms of propulsion.

Materials

1 micro:bit, 1 USB cable & 1 battery pack, 1 large plastic soda bottle, 1 cork, bicycle valve, tape, scissors, water, bicycle pump, a plastic crate with at least one hole large enough to hold the mouth of a soda bottle, utility knife, nail, safety glasses.

Caution!

Be careful when you launch the rocket and do not lean over it while you are pumping it up. Make sure your friends stand far away. Wearing safety googles is recommended.

Make

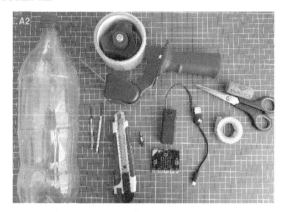

1. Assemble your materials

2. Cut the cork in half.

3. Make sure the cork fits tightly in the bottle.

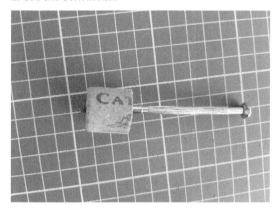

4. Drill a hole all the way through the cork with a sharp nail.

5. Insert a bicycle valve into the cork. Check to be sure that air flows all the way through the valve and cork.

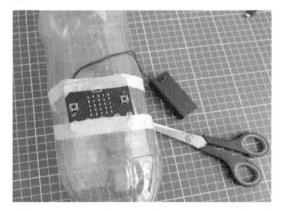

6. Tape the micro:bit and battery box onto the plastic bottle. Secure everything carefully so you don't lose it when the rocket launches!

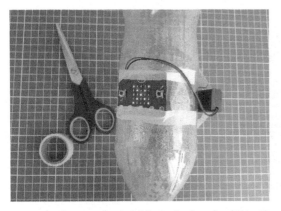

7. Create the program in MakeCode, download it to the micro:bit, and test the system by lifting and lowering your rocket by hand.

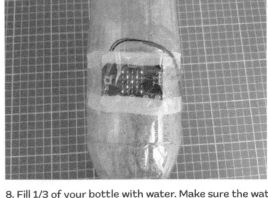

8. Fill 1/3 of your bottle with water. Make sure the water does not leak and your electronic components stay dry.

9. Connect the bicycle valve to the pump.

10. Install your rocket on the launch platform. When ready, press A to start running the micro:bit code.

11. Pump as hard as you can to increase the air pressure within the bottle. Eventually, it should blast off!

12. After the rocket touches down, Press B on the micro:bit to display how long the rocket was going up.

The Invent to Learn Guide to the micro:bit

Tips

- Keep the micro:bit dry at all times!
- A plastic crate works well as a launch platform.
- Make sure that your micro:bit and battery are securely connected to your rocket. Losing the battery box or micro:bit will be expensive and ruin your experiment.
- There is a video of this build on microbit.inventtolearn.com.

Program - Liftoff

In this part of the program, you will set up your rocket for liftoff and create the code to display the duration of its upward flight once it lands.

Let's begin by creating the code for setting up the project's initial values and variables and program the A and B buttons to behave like a stopwatch.

- Create the following code in MakeCode.
- Before you create the blocks below, you will need to create five new variables for **liftoff**, **freefall**, **start**, **starttime**, and **endtime**.
- You will need five versions of the `set` block found in the **Variables** panel. Use the dropdown arrow to select each variable. Set all their initial values to false or zero as shown, indicating that the flight has not started yet.

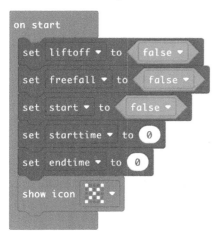

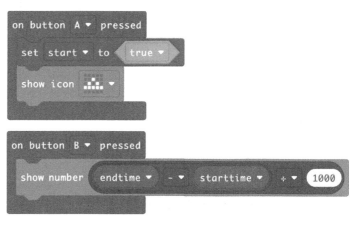

- In the `on button B` block, add a `show number` block. Then drag in a divide operator from the **Math** panel of the Toolbox. The subtraction math operator is placed inside the divide operator. Finally, drag the variables, **endtime** and **starttime** into the subtraction operator.
- Name the project *Rocket*, and save the code.

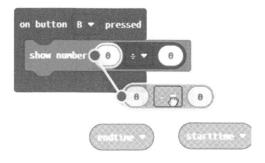

Understanding the code - Liftoff

The `on start` block initializes the important variables in the project code. This process is common to a lot of programming contexts when you need to do things like initialize a score or reposition an object before your program begins. Imagine a game in which the score doesn't start at zero, the rules are unfair, or the game is over instantly. That would not be much fun to play. In this case, we need to initialize variables in order to trigger events in the larger program and keep track of how long your rocket is in flight.

When you press the A button, the rocket is set to begin timing its ascent. The timer will begin as soon as pumping the bicycle pump causes liftoff.

When the B button is pressed, the elapsed time of the ascent is displayed in seconds. (This will not actually work until we build the Timer code.)

Do you know why we are dividing the time by 1,000?

Icons are displayed on the micro:bit to signify readiness and liftoff.

Programming - Timer

Next, build the rest of the code for the rocket project. The timer will record the duration of the ascent of the rocket. Once 3G of force is detected by the rocket blasting off, a timer begins counting its climb. Once the rocket reaches its peak altitude, it begins free-falling back to earth and causes the micro:bit to stop recording the elapsed time.

- Add the following code to your MakeCode project
- Save the project

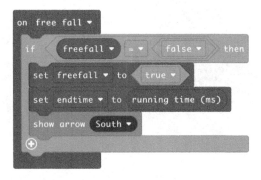

Note: The `running time (ms)` block is found in the **... more** section of the **Input** blocks.

`on 3g` and `on free fall` are all options in the `on shake` block found in the **Input** blocks.

Understanding the code - Timer

Once you press the A button the code will wait for liftoff to begin the timer.

Once the rocket launches, the program waits until it detects 3g of force (in the `on 3g` block) and then changes the state of **liftoff** to **true** and records the **starttime** by setting it to the clock value reported by the block, `running time (ms)`.

The code in the `on 3g` block is a bit tricky since you only want the program to start the timer once and the micro:bit may detect 3 or more gs of force many times. This is why it's important to set and check the **true/false** state of the **liftoff** and **start** variables.

The `running time (ms)` is a built-in function of the micro:bit that starts counting from the moment the micro:bit is turned on.

The code for the `on free fall` block behaves in a similar fashion to the `on 3g` block. The micro:bit detects when it begins falling, sets the value of **freefall** to **true** and records the **endtime**.

Arrows are displayed on the micro:bit to indicate ascent or descent.

Test your rocket

Test your code by tossing your rocket and letting it fall carefully. If you can see the micro:bit display, the arrows should change from up to down. Press B to see how long your rocket was in the air.

Time to blast off!

- Position the rocket on the launch platform.
- Put on your safety goggles and ask all of your friends to back away from the rocket.
- Press the A button on the micro:bit.
- Pump the bicycle pump for liftoff. Do not lean over the bottle or hold the bottle as you pump.
- Retrieve the rocket, press the B button on the micro:bit, and see how long the rocket climbed before its descent.

Challenges

- If you are using a micro:bit V2, play a sound to indicate that it is falling.
- Try more or less water in your rocket.
- Can you program a second micro:bit to display the flight information recorded by the rocket? You might also use the second micro:bit instead of pressing the A and B buttons on the micro:bit attached to the rocket and radio blocks.
- Record the flight times of multiple attempts to calculate an average time aloft.
- Compete against friends' pumping skill and rocket designs to see whose rocket can fly the longest.
- Can you propel a rocket by mixing vinegar and baking soda instead of using the air pump? Be sure to protect the micro:bit from getting wet!

micro:bit Resources

Further Adventures with the micro:bit

micro:bit Coding Options

Resources & Books

micro:bit Power Possibilities

The micro:bit Goes to School

Supported by Learning Theories

Lesson Planning Resources

Stream Your MakeCode Lesson

Manage Student Projects with the micro:bit Classroom

Why This Book Matters

Material Gallery

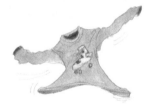

About the Authors

Also from Constructing Modern Knowledge Press

micro:bit Resources

Further Adventures with the micro:bit

Wishing to supercharge micro:bit projects? Go beyond three pin connectors? Add more sensors and motors? These products will allow kids to continue learning now and well into the future.

bit:booster

Lectrify.it

The bit:booster is a Swiss-Army knife for expanding the functionality of the BBC micro:bit. Plug in the micro:bit and gain use of many more pins with easy-to-connect ports. The bit:booster also allows users to connect toy (DC) motors, LEGO motors, and Grove sensors. Its on-board battery pack provides enough power for several servos at once. The bit:booster also features programmable NeoPixels and can power an OLED display. Kids will put this low-cost expansion board to use immediately.

Servo:Lite board

kitronik.co.uk

The low-cost Servo:Lite board from the fantastic micro:bit accessory company, Kitronik, features five programmable NeoPixels, and a 3 AAA battery pack to power up to three servos simultaneously. Kitronik ships worldwide quickly and provides great customer support. They are a great source of micro:bit add-on boards and electronic components for education.

Hummingbird Bit Robotics Kit

Birdbraintechnologies.com

The Hummingbird Robotics Kit uses the micro:bit as the brain for a robotics platform that allows children to create a wide range of interactive physical computing projects. The kit comes with rotation (360) and position (180) servos, LEDS, tricolor LEDs, and sensors for detecting sound, light, temperature, distance, and rotation. Motors, lights, and sensors connect easily and securely with spring loaded terminals. Best of all, the Hummingbird Robotics Kit may be programmed in many languages, including Snap!, Python, MakeCode, Java, microBlocks, and Swift on Mac, Windows, iOS, and Android. This is a powerhouse product for supporting classroom projects.

Lectrify, Kitronik, and BirdBrain Technologies have web sites filled with project ideas, teacher tips, and technical support.

Vendors

These vendors carry many different micro:bit parts and accessories. Some of their websites feature extensive micro:bit tutorials and lessons.

Boards, kits, and more

Sparkfun Electronics – Specializes in hobbyist electronic components, tools, and kits. sparkfun.com

Adafruit – Unique and fun DIY electronics and kits. adafruit.com

Kitronik – Makes and sells electronic project kits for micro:bit, e-textiles, robotics, and other maker needs. UK-based. kitronik.co.uk

Lectrify – Easy to use electronic parts and micro:bit add-ons that make all connections easier – sewing, soldering, or clips. Lessons and projects introduce circuits to any grade level. lectrify.it

DF Robot – Carries many micro:bit kits and accessories. Ships worldwide from Shanghai. dfrobot.com

4 Tronix – A variety of micro:bit kits from many manufacturers. UK based. shop.4tronix.co.uk

micro:bit Foundation list of resellers – A continuously updated, comprehensive list of global sources for boards, kits, and accessories. These links can be accessed from the Help icon on the upper right of the MakeCode interface. microbit.org/buy and microbit.org/buy/accessories

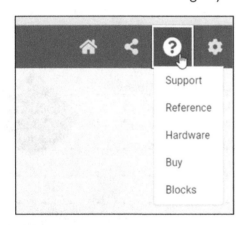

Good for components

Digikey – Extensive collection of electronic components. digikey.com

Electronics Goldmine – Huge supply of cheap electronic parts. Look for deals and bulk purchases, for example, a container of 200 LEDs for $5.00. goldmine-elec-products.com

Jaycar – Australian supplier of electronic components. jaycar.com.au or jaycar.us

Jameco Electronics – A popular source of electronics parts and kits. jameco.com

Amazon & eBay – There are often good deals to be found, but be cautious and read the fine print. EBay is a good source for bulk components like LEDs and batteries. amazon.com and ebay.com

micro:bit Coding Options

Most of the projects in this book are programmed with MakeCode, but there are many options for coding with the micro:bit.

MakeCode

makecode.com

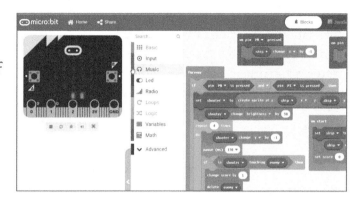

The MakeCode block environment is one of the easiest ways to program your micro:bit. Start with basics, explore advanced functions, or add extensions. You can also switch from coding in blocks to coding in JavaScript or Python. Once finished, connect and download your code easily to your micro:bit. You can even share your code online or publish on github.

micro:bit app

microbit.org/get-started/user-guide/mobile

A micro:bit app is available for your mobile phone or tablet. In many ways it resembles MakeCode. You program on the phone or tablet and send your code to the micro:bit with Bluetooth.

Scratch

scratch.mit.edu

On the Scratch website, you can add special micro:bit blocks to enable micro:bit projects in Scratch. At the time of publication, only some of the micro:bit sensors can be used in Scratch. This book features two projects that use Scratch to program the micro:bit, *A Spooky Game in Scratch* and *Race Car Game Controller in Scratch*.

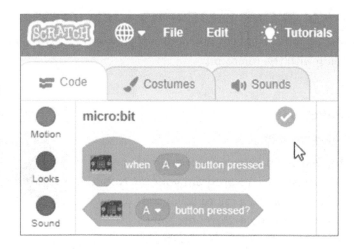

MicroBlocks

microblocks.fun

MicroBlocks is a block-based programming language for physical computing. It runs on a number of microcontrollers including the micro:bit.

MicroBlocks is a live coding environment. Programs run immediately without waiting or downloading.

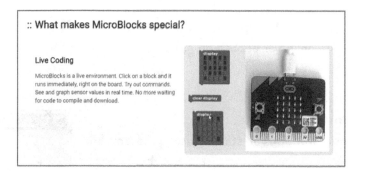

MakeCode app for Windows

The MakeCode Windows app is available for free in the Microsoft Store. You can work offline to write micro:bit programs. The app uses the same block environment as the MakeCode website.

Python or JavaScript

MakeCode allows you to program the micro:bit with blocks, Python, or JavaScript. Python and JavaScript are text-based languages used by hobbyists and professionals. Text-based programming is often trickier than blocks because there are grammatical rules you need to follow, including the specific use of punctuation. Block-based languages reduce or eliminate these details.

Select the language you wish to use by clicking the menu above the work area in MakeCode. Blocks easily convert to Python or JavaScript code, but the transition from text-based code to blocks may be messier or not work at all since your text-based code may be more complicated.

Python and JavaScript are both popular for creating interactive web sites and software applications. Python is typically thought of as being easier to learn. Python programs are executed (run) on the server side of the network while JavaScript programs run right in the browser. That makes JavaScript a faster and more robust language for Web applications.

You can also use JavaScript to write custom extensions for MakeCode and publish those to GitHub.

MicroPython for micro:bit

python.microbit.org

This is a text-based environment to program your micro:bit with more functionality than MakeCode Python offers. For example, MicroPython offers text to speech. In this book, there is a project in MicroPython where you can make the micro:bit talk, *Talking micro:bit in Python*.

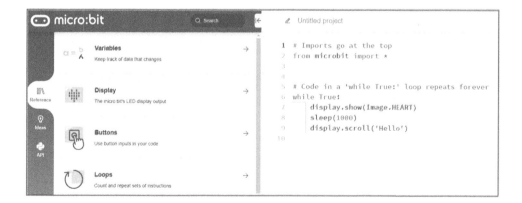

Tinkercad
tinkercad.com

Many people use Tinkercad to design 3D printed objects. Tinkercad can also be used to program the micro:bit and design electronics that attach to micro:bit pins. The Tinkercad simulator allows more complex electronic design than MakeCode alone. Tinkercad also offers programming in both MakeCode and Python. Tinkercad Classrooms is useful for sharing and commenting on designs.

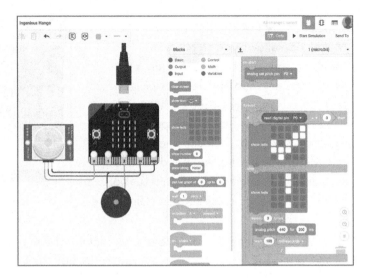

micro:bit app vendors

In the iOS app store and Google Play you will find different apps for the micro:bit designed by vendors to interface with devices such as motor boards and robots.

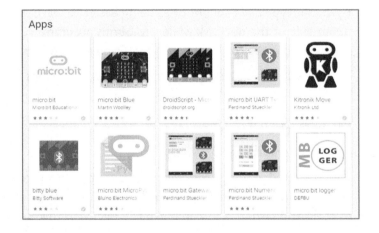

Resources & Books

There is a growing body of resources available to support the micro:bit.

The Basics

The micro:bit Foundation is a non-profit organization supporting the BBC micro:bit and its millions of users worldwide. There are resources for students, teachers, developers, and an online community. This is a website you should fully explore! microbit.org

The micro:bit Go Kit is the easiest way to get started with micro:bit. For around $15 (US) you get a micro:bit, battery box, 2 AA batteries, and USB cable. Find these kits at the vendors mentioned in this book or microbit.org/buy

Online Resources

Micro:bit projects and tutorials

The micro:bit Foundation site offers a variety of lessons and projects for the micro:bit microbit.org/lessons and microbit.org/projects

Getting Started with micro:bit is an online tutorial from Sparkfun for the BBC micro:bit. learn.sparkfun.com/tutorials/getting-started-with-the-microbit

BBC micro:bit Kitronik University has extensive online tutorials, projects at all levels, and teaching resources for the BBC micro:bit. Kitronik is a UK-based vendor and also a partner in the development of teaching materials and expansion boards for the UK Design and Technology curriculum for Year 7 students. kitronik.co.uk/blog/bbc-microbit-kitronik-university

EU CodeWeek website offers three downloadable projects with extensive resources for the micro:bit that support students in language, math, and other subjects. Choose from Morse Code (for primary students), Escape Room (for lower secondary students), or Making an Automaton (for upper secondary students) Morse Code with the micro: bit, for Primary School. These projects are translated into 27 languages. codeweek.eu/training/making-an-automaton-with-microbit

do your :bit is an annual, worldwide challenge organized by the micro:bit Foundation to develop world-changing ideas using the micro:bit that are based on the United Nations Sustainable Development Goals (SDGs). microbit.org/projects/do-your-bit/

Micro:bit hackster from the Micro:bit Educational Foundation has a wide variety of easy to follow project tutorials to make with your micro:bit. microbit.hackster.io

Microbit101 is a Dutch site and Instagram account (@microbit101) by the authors of this book with 101 project to make and code with your micro:bit. Lots of tinkering and tutorials how to make your projects. microbit101.nl

Arduino IDE for micro:bit – Follow this detailed tutorial from Adafruit to use the Arduino IDE to program the micro:bit. It's a bit complicated (but not difficult) and you will be able to use the global library of Arduino sketches as a start for your micro:bit project. learn.adafruit.com/use-micro-bit-with-arduino/overview

Learning to code

Almost all of the coding options for the micro:bit offer tutorials, sample projects, and helpful resources.

MakeCode - On the MakeCode website you find tutorials and sample projects for beginners and experts. makecode.microbit.org

MakeCode project starters - Project starter cards for math concepts and games are available at makecode.microbit.org/coding-cards

Scratch micro:bit coding cards - Free printable coding cards designed to support Scratch-based micro:bit projects. microbit.org/scratch and scratch.mit.edu/microbit

Python micro:bit resources - Lots of Python projects for your micro:bit. headstartacademy.com.au/python-microbit-resources

Social media

Explore social media and video sites like FaceBook, Twitter, Instagram, TikTok, and YouTube to find many micro:bit related groups, projects, and tutorials.

Print resources

Magazines

Micro:bit magazine – Free online magazine about the BBC micro:bit. You can purchase print editions at micromag.cc

micro:mag – A free online magazine with fun projects and practical tips for the micro:bit. You can purchase the print versions. magazines.micromag.cc

Guidebooks

Getting Started with the BBC Micro:Bit by Mike Tooley. A good introductory book.

The Official BBC micro:bit User Guide by Gareth Halfacree. A comprehensive guide.

Project books

micro:bit in Wonderland: Coding & Craft with the BBC micro:bit by Tracy Gardner & Elibrie de Kock. All the projects are related to the story of Alice in Wonderland.

Save the World with Code by Lorraine Underwood. This book has twenty fun projects that can each be made with either the micro:bit, an Adafruit Circuit Playground Express, or the Raspberry Pi.

Micro:bit for Mad Scientists: 30 Clever Coding and Electronics Projects for Kids by Simon Monk. Thirty science projects and experiments to make with the micro:bit. There are projects using both MakeCode and Python.

The Tinkerer's Guide to the micro:bit Galaxy by Tinkercademy. The twenty projects in this book show you how to add motors, LEDs, relays, and more to the micro:bit.

Scrappy Circuits by Michael Carroll. While not specifically a book about micro:bits, Scrappy Circuits shows you how to make simple DIY electronic projects and games with parts from the dollar store, office supplies, and found items (also known as junk). Dozens of fun projects and frugal tips will help you learn electronics as you build even more micro:bit projects.

micro:bit Power Possibilities

The micro:bit needs power. When connected to a computer, your micro:bit gets power from the computer through the USB cable. When you unplug the micro:bit from your computer, you must supply power another way. This is usually done with a battery pack, but there are other options. **Caution!** The micro:bit needs 3 volts, and should not be connected to anything with more power than that unless that accessory is specifically made for the micro:bit.

A standard micro:bit battery pack uses 2 AA batteries. Unplug the cable or remove a battery when you are done. When pulling the battery cable out of the micro:bit, grasp the plastic connector. Do not pull the wires.

This battery pack has a on and off switch which makes it easier to turn your project off when you are done.

The MI-Power board uses a 3 volt CR 2032 coin cell battery. A variety of companies make coin cell battery boards like this.

There are many different kinds of motor and extension boards for the micro:bit that provide the increased power needed to power motors without harming the micro:bit.

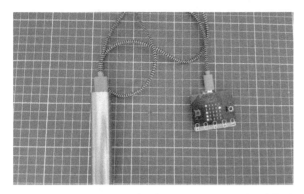

You can use a USB power bank to power your micro:bit. A long cable is convenient for your maker projects in order to hide the power bank.

Of course you can keep the micro-USB cable connected to your computer to power a micro:bit.

Use a USB power plug (like a phone charger) to provide power to your micro:bit. Your project will have to stay close to an electric outlet.

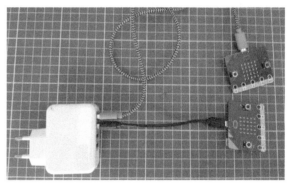

You can use a USB power hub to power multiple micro:bits for a project. Long cables are really useful for this.

Tips

- If you use rechargeable batteries, check their voltage before use. While rechargeable batteries are good for the environment, some of them have higher voltage output than the micro:bit can handle.
- If motors or lights begin to misbehave, it could be because your batteries are running low.
- When you are done, unplug the power source from your micro:bit.
- While testing code, keep the micro:bit connected to your computer.

The micro:bit Goes to School

The micro:bit is an excellent way to solve problems, invent things, and learn about computer science. Using digital technology that interacts with the world is also called "physical computing" and can be found in such real-world products from robots to wearable technology, and many more. It supports the integration of subject areas, especially in Science, Technology, Engineering, and Math (STEM). Projects that include a micro:bit have an added benefit of using design, often represented by adding and A (for Art & Design) to STEM subjects making it STEAM!

You can create projects large and small, work together in groups or individually, connect projects to curriculum, or just have fun! Along the way, learning happens as a natural outcome of young people having experiences that are meaningful and relevant, with opportunities to think hard and do real things.

Supported by Learning Theories

There are many educational theories that support the idea that real experiences lead to real learning. Here are just a few.

Jean Piaget - Psychologist

Students are naturally enthusiastic and will quickly learn the basics of the micro:bit. But if you really want them to actually make things, you have to take it step by step. Jean Piaget is an important psychologist who studied the development of children. Piaget theorized that there are four stages of development in learning:

- Sensorimotor (feel and touch)
- Pre-operational (research and try)
- Specifically operational (logical connections)
- Formally operational (abstract thinking)

Stages 1 and 2 will be easy with the micro:bit, but if you start to make more complex projects, you will need to do a bit of planning and start to make the logical connections needed to go deeper. The Design Canvas is a way for students to think about their projects before they start, developing skills in planning and design.

Seymour Papert - Mathematician

Seymour Papert was a mathematician who worked with Piaget to help him to understand how children construct mathematical knowledge. Papert was fascinated by the work of Piaget and he started to tinker with computers because he saw them not just a way adults could do work, but as an intellectual laboratory for children. In 1967 at the Massachusetts Institute of Technology (MIT), Papert with Cynthia Solomon and Wally Feurzig, invented the first programming language for children, Logo. Logo is the basis for Scratch and many other programming languages used around the world to support learning. Papert's genius was to create mathematical tools that children could learn naturally, a powerful idea even today.

Jeanette Wing - Professor of computer science

Jeanette Wing popularized the term, "computational thinking" in 2006. "Computational thinking is the thought processes involved in formulating a problem and expressing its solution(s) in such a way that a computer—human or machine—can effectively carry out." In short, learning to solve problems as a computer does is a skill that is very useful in today's world. No matter what programming language you learn, there are worthwhile skills you will learn like breaking the problem into parts, recognizing patterns, creating algorithms, and debugging.

Gary Stager and Sylvia Martinez - Teacher educators

Invent to Learn: Making, Tinkering, and Engineering in the Classroom (2013, second edition 2019). It is known as the "bible" for the maker movement in schools. *Invent to Learn* builds on many ideas not just from Piaget and Papert, but also from Leonardo da Vinci to Mr. Rogers. *Invent to Learn* translates these ideas into practical suggestions for teachers to implement project-based learning with modern technology in real classrooms. Often the process of making is difficult for teachers to implement in the curriculum, but Sylvia and Gary show how it can be done.

Lesson Planning Resources

What is the best age to introduce students to the micro:bit?

In most cases the ideal age for introducing the micro:bit is around 10 years old. When you start too early with the micro:bit, students may not be able to make the logical connections and do the necessary abstract thinking. However, younger students can be successful, especially if they have already have experience with Scratch, or have an adult or older peer at hand to guide them and to help with some of the harder parts, like the downloading and pairing.

Students who have some experience with Scratch will likely find that using MakeCode is quite similar and can easily make that adjustment. Do not feel that you must first use the micro:bit with Scratch, and then introduce MakeCode. In fact, using Scratch can sometimes be more frustrating because it only uses a fraction of the micro:bit's potential.

Age of Students				
Hardware	BeeBot	Lego WeDo	micro:bit	micro:bit & accessories	Arduino/ Raspberry Pi
Software	Scratch JR	Scratch	MakeCode	JavaScript, Python, micro Python	Arduino/ Raspberry Pi

Planning micro:bit Projects

Think, Make, & Improve

In *Invent to Learn*, Gary Stager and Sylvia Martinez introduce a simple structure for planning and working on projects called "Think, Make, Improve." Once your students gain a basic understanding of the micro:bit, and their projects grow in complexity, you can introduce them to this planning process.

Design Canvas

We designed a template we call the Design Canvas that you can use for students to write down what they are going to make, think about how they are going to make it and keep working at it. Once they try something, one of two things generally happen:

1. They find a bug or it doesn't quite work as expected—they need to fix something.

2. It works, but they might have an idea to make it better.

This is not to say this all gets written down ahead of time! The template should be a useful tool, not a hurdle to making their projects awesome.

You can download this template from microbit.inventtolearn.com.

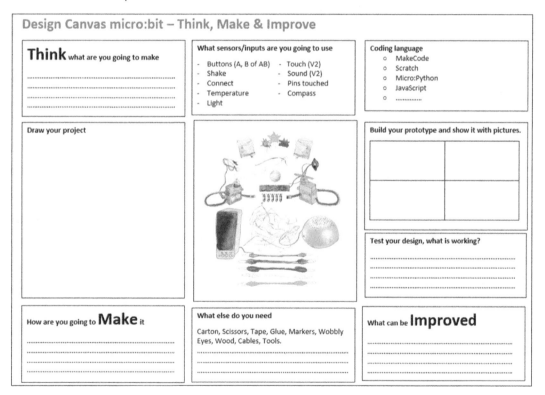

Using the projects in this book to support learning

If students have an idea of what to make, they can use projects in this book as a starting point. The more projects your students make with these guided tutorials, the better they will understand how to make something unique themselves. Honor the differences in their approaches—some may like to make the projects exactly like they are in the book, whereas others may just take the ideas. Some might want to start with the easiest, others with the more difficult projects. All these approaches are valid. Make sure that all attempts are celebrated, and that there is no failure, only hurdles to be overcome.

Sample student projects

These projects were made by 10-12 year olds at a school in the Netherlands (CBS de Hoeksteen in Spijkenisse) who worked in teams for five weeks with the Design Canvas.

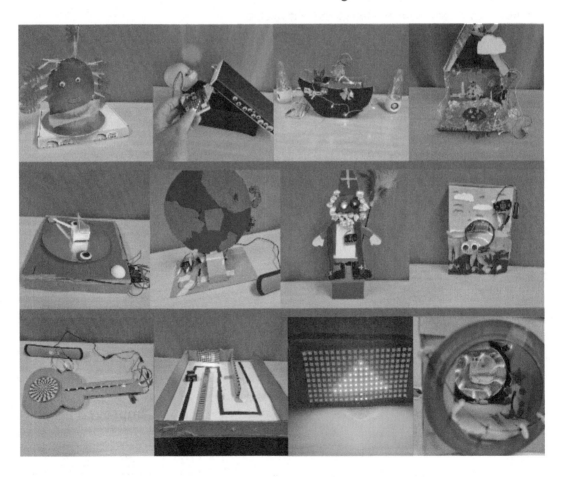

A sample unit plan for an introduction to the micro:bit

Use this outline and the projects in this book as a guide for an 8-10 week unit. This outline is designed for a weekly class of about 40 minutes, so adjust accordingly for your own timeline and schedule.

Introduction to the micro:bit		
The basics	1 session	Use the projects in the *Warm Ups* Section to introduce the basics. With minimal lecturing, get them hands-on as quickly as possible. The students will learn the basics of the micro:bit, how to put the code on the micro:bit, and how to navigate in the online programming environment of MakeCode. It is useful to have students work in pairs so they can talk out loud through their problems.
Try some projects	3 -5 sessions	Each session, choose one project from the *Getting Started* or the *It's Alive* section and ask your students to make it. Try these projects yourself ahead of time to make sure you have the right materials and know how they work. As the students recreate the projects, it gives them a solid foundation in hardware and software. The students should work in groups with a maximum of three students.
Invent something!	3 sessions	Ask the students to make a project of their own choosing. They can use the Design Canvas, but they should have an idea they can start working on right away. This is an opportunity to add in requirements as you see fit—for example, curriculum connections, or specific technical requirements like using sensors or motors. They might work in small groups with a maximum of four students.
Show off	1 session	In this session, students will show off their work. The format of this can vary widely: presentations, making a movie, a gallery walk, invite parents and the community, open it to the rest of the school, or invite the local TV news! Students should be prepared to present their project and what they might improve the next time.

Unplugged MakeCode blocks

Sometimes it is useful to have a set of large MakeCode blocks printed out. Use these blocks to explain code to students or allow students to use them as they think about the code they want to create. Find large printable versions of the basic micro:bit blocks in a downloadable file on the resource website for this book microbit.inventtolearn.com.

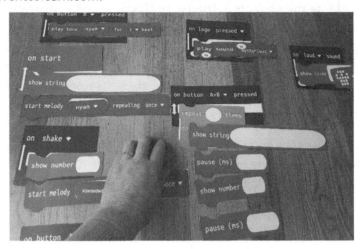

Power teaching tip

For classroom demonstrations, replace the short micro-USB cable used by the micro:bit with one at least a meter long. This lets you hold the micro:bit high enough for the whole class to see it. Be sure to buy a cable that connects your computer on one end (USB or USB-C) to micro-USB on the other.

Student experts

If you have students with mixed abilities or experience with Scratch, teach students to be class experts so they can help others. Teach them how to teach—that is, they should not grab someone's mouse and do it themselves, but lead others to solutions.

Remote teaching with the micro:bit

Remote teaching with the micro:bit is easy with the MakeCode Streamer (makecode.com/streamer) and the Classroom tool (classroom.microbit.org). Read more about these useful tools in the following pages.

If remote teaching means your students don't have access to the micro:bit board every day, they can still do coding projects using the MakeCode Simulator. But of course it is more fun with the micro:bit and tinkering material.

Stream MakeCode Lessons

MakeCode Streamer (makecode.com/streamer) is a web application that simplifies the creation of interactive, high-quality coding support videos. Streamer incorporates a live MakeCode screen, video, audio, and screen paint tools into a recorded video or even to broadcast live streaming.

Streamer is designed for teachers, students, or anyone who wants to make videos that combine MakeCode coding with instruction or explanation.

You can use Streamer for a remote lesson, or to make tutorials for your students explaining a bit of code or a whole project. You can appear in the video, and even add an extra camera showing how your micro:bit works in your project.

Students could use Streamer to record a project presentation, or to create a "how to" video for others to view.

1. Go to makecode.com/streamer. You may need to give permission for MakeCode to access your camera.

2. In the lower right corner, you will see yourself on the screen. If you click on the small icon, you can change the settings. You can put yourself in the left or right corner and make your image larger.

3. When you move your mouse across the bottom of the screen, extra functions will appear.

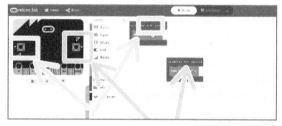

4. You can draw arrows, rectangles, change the colors, and add accents. If you press the exit all the drawings will disappear.

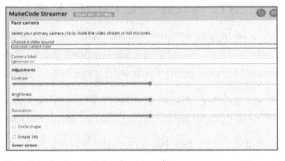

5. At the right top of the screen another toolbar controls functions like full screen, captions, record, and settings.

6. In Settings, you can change editor camera settings.

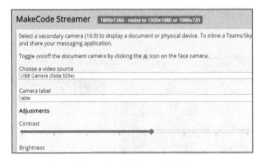

7. You can use a green screen or change it to any color you like!

8. Settings is also where you can add an extra camera.

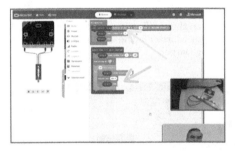

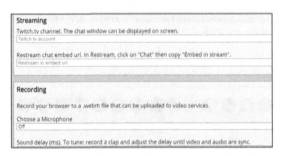

9. Use the extra camera to show how to connect your micro:bit to external devices, and how the code works.

10. You can record your whole session, including the coding in action, your video and audio, and your external camera, and even stream it.

Tips

- MakeCode Streamer documentation: makecode.com/streamer/docs
- The best way to learn to do this is to try something!
- Buy a simple USB camera to use in your sessions. You can use your laptop camera, but an extra camera allows you to show what is on your desk.

Manage Student Projects with Classroom

The micro:bit Foundation has developed a Classroom website (classroom.microbit.org) where you (as a teacher) can easily share your own code and see your students' work in progress. You may create any number of classrooms and give students joining details so they can see any code you share. The Dashboard gives you a view of student progress and even their live code.

The micro:bit Classroom is an excellent tool for remote learning.

Set up your Classroom

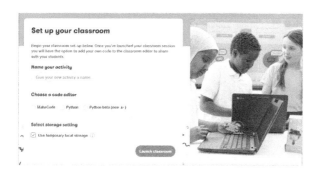

1. Go to classroom.microbit.org

2. Set up your Classroom by giving your activity a name. Choose which programming language you want. Then **Launch classroom**.

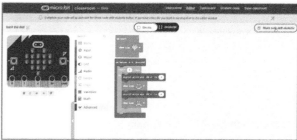

3. On the next page you will see the four steps to make and manage your classroom project. Select **Editor** on top of the site to make any code you want to share with students.

4. Make your code and select **Share code with students** at the right top corner.

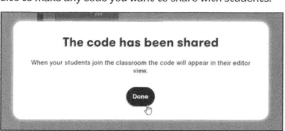

5. Select **Done** and your code will be shared with your students.

6. Select **Dashboard** to access the joining details to share with your students. Once they join you can see their code.

Tips

- Work is not saved online between sessions, but you can download it all and restart at a future time. Think of this more like activities, rather than a whole semester-long class.
- When you do this for the first time, prepare your starting code in advance.
- Watch the online tutorial for more ideas about using the Classroom.
- You can show your students' code to give other students tips about how to solve their coding problems.

Managing your Classroom

1. Now you have the Classroom joining details for your students to login. You can make your starting code in advance and share it with your students at the start of your lesson.

2. Your students will login on microbit.org/join with the Classroom joining details.

3. The student will fill in their name and select continue.

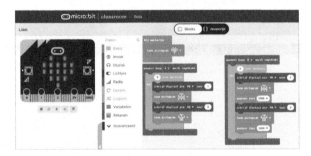

4. Your students will get your start code and can make changes.

5. You as a teacher can see the students who have joined the micro:bit classroom website.

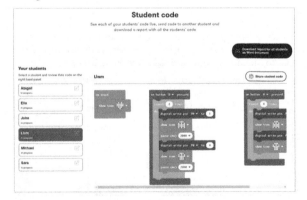

6. If you select a student, you can see what they are coding in real time.

7. If a student is finished they can select I've **finished** and send you their micro:bit code.

8. In your list of students, you can see which students are finished.

9. As the teacher, you can download the code to a Microsoft Word document. Or you can select **Save classroom** in the right top corner.

10. If you want to save the classroom and continue the next time, select **Save classroom file** and it will download all your student data to a HTML file on your computer. Next time you can open this file and select **Resume**. Your students will get a new login code and can continue their work.

Why This Book Matters

By Gary Stager

Millions of the miraculous low-cost microcontroller development board, the BBC micro:bit, are in use across the globe. This new book takes a comprehensive approach to teaching children to make and code exciting interactive projects using the micro:bit as its "brain board"—expanding the range of what often happens in classrooms.

The Invent to Learn Guide to the micro:bit combines coding, craft, and creativity to teach physical computing, engineering, computer science, and electronics to students in grades 4-9. Authors Pauline Maas and Peter Heldens designed whimsical projects sure to delight a wide variety of kids while teaching important computing and engineering concepts.

The Invent to Learn Guide to the micro:bit is built upon the intellectual traditions of project-based learning and constructionism. Readers are provided with just enough inspiration and explanation to make projects, and the resulting knowledge, their own. This book can be used by students, but may also be used as a resource for creative teachers looking for project inspiration or as the basis for a course of study.

Projects matter

I may be biased, but *The Invent to Learn Guide to the micro:bit* is the gold standard in books about robotics, programming, and engineering for children. The book is not only distinguished by the ways in which it expands the range of what's possible in classrooms, but also in the approach it takes to teaching S.T.E.M. concepts to children (and their teachers).

Most projects in *The Invent to Learn Guide to the micro:bit* use Microsoft MakeCode as their programming environment and treat "Make Code" literally. Each project in the book includes a making component and computer coding to make things happen. Every project employs one or more micro:bits. Young inventors are invited to embellish, personalize, add creative touches, and expand the functionality of each project via computer programming, art, and design.

> *This book's ingenious projects celebrate the culture of childhood.*

Too many "maker" books suffer by speeding from simple to impossible within a few pages. Others promise robotics or tinkering but deliver arts and crafts. This book is different. The projects increase in complexity gradually and are developmentally appropriate. Every project requires construction and coding. This broadens the appeal for a diverse population of children. Reader-tinkerers are encouraged to tackle increasingly sophisticated projects and personalize them. There are plenty of challenges presented for high-flyers, giving kids a good look at the micro:bits remarkable functionality and their own potential.

Playing with powerful concepts

A common pedagogical error is made by many educators using computers in the classroom who believe it is important to learn all the menu options and features of a software package. As a result, some teachers require students to memorize such technical details, often without ever using the functionality being studied. This is not only a waste of time, but exactly the wrong strategy, especially when using web-based software that is likely to change and be upgraded over time, like MakeCode. The most practical approach to use software like MakeCode is to understand it conceptually. When such fluency develops, you can find the tool or feature you need, regardless of the current interface. Such skills transfer more readily to different coding environments as well.

Occasionally, the book casually introduces new programming concepts with little or no explanation. Subsequent projects utilizing that concept are accompanied by more explanation. This choice represents a deliberate pedagogical stance. The priority should be rich experience over rhetoric. Piaget teaches us that "knowledge is a consequence of experience." Action concretizes the learning process. For example, using a "random" block in the fortune teller project creates an opportunity for "messing about" with the mathematically significant concept of randomness in a natural playful fashion. No long explanation is required.

This book's ingenious projects celebrate the culture of childhood. Critical skills are developed without straining them through the antiseptic lens of vocational training or increasing test scores. Playful does not mean simple or mindless. The book seeks to democratize computer science and physical computing by appealing to a wide variety of students and teachers.

The projects in *The Invent to Learn Guide to the micro:bit* demonstrate powerful computational ideas while requiring problem solving and persistence. In fact, I am unaware of another text about MakeCode programming that introduces more computing concepts to children. Readers will deal with loops, variables, conditionals, sensory inputs, actuator output, timing, synchronization, parallelism, randomness, inequality, procedurality, radio communication, data collection and analysis, coordinates, plus a host of other computer science concepts situated within a project approach.

Students are also invited to explore engineering principles, design, simple electronics, precision, motors, lights, sensors, inputs, friction, mechanical advantage, and a host of other physical science concepts. Rather than being reduced to a list of vocabulary words, these powerful ideas on the frontier of modernity come alive when learners are engaged in playful, meaningful, and creative projects.

Debugging – a 21st century skill

This book is based on a conviction that children and their teachers are competent. They are capable of reproducing block-based computer programs accurately—a contemporary literacy skill. When something does not work with their physical model or computer program, debugging is required. Debugging develops critical habits of mind. Its importance cannot be overstated. Seymour Papert, one of the inventors of Logo, the first programming language for children, said:

> *Many children are held back in their learning because they have a model of learning in which you have either 'got it' or 'got it wrong.' But when you program a computer you almost never get it right the first time. Learning to be a master programmer is learning to become highly skilled at isolating and correcting bugs... The question to ask about the program is not whether it is right or wrong, but if it is fixable. If this way of looking at intellectual products were generalized to how the larger culture thinks about knowledge and its acquisition we might all be less intimidated by our fears of "being wrong" (Papert, 1980).*

A book filled with links to someone else's code may provide the illusion of efficiency but does so at the expense of learning. Creating short block-based programs manually is not a great burden for children. It encourages them to develop fluency in the software environment, read the code, predict its behavior, and become more skilled debuggers when inevitable errors crop up.

Physical computing

Physical computing is the product of making things and programming. The projects in this book move beyond arts and craft projects to add intelligence and interactivity to one's inventions.

Computer programming perfectly matches a young person's remarkable capacity for intensity and yet far too few students learn to program in school. Programming experiences turn the computer into an intellectual laboratory and vehicle for self-expression. Schools have long overvalued learning with one's head while the future requires learning with one's heart, hands, and head equally. Regardless of the path today's student follows, they will be required to solve problems that involve making things out of bits or atoms. The projects in this book require both and are designed to appeal to a wide variety of tastes, styles, and interests.

Small but mighty

The micro:bit is a new species of technology, the microcontroller development board (MDB). Like other microcontrollers such as Arduino, the micro:bit is a little brainboard featuring pins for inputs and outputs. Sensors report information to the embedded microprocessor. The program you write decides what to do with that information and then produces a result by sending instructions to lights, motors, speakers, displays, or other devices. This is achieved by creating circuitry connecting input and output devices to the microcontroller, usually via breadboards or soldering.

A microcontroller development board, such as the micro:bit, has input and output features built right into the board. This lowers the barrier to entry by reducing costs, confusion, and complexity for beginners while offering sufficient power for advanced projects. While you can and will learn a bit about electronics working with the micro:bit, all of the messy bits about circuitry, voltage, resistance, and more have disappeared. Thanks to the micro:bit, novices can have their first physical computing projects built and programmed within minutes.

For many reasons, the micro:bit may be the physical computing platform of choice in schools for the next decade.

Software matters!

For the past decade, the widely popular family of Arduino microcontrollers has been the choice for simple physical computing projects. However, for educators hoping to introduce students to these powerful concepts, the software used for programming the Arduino is a high hurdle—difficult to learn and use. Many young programmers simply repurpose pieces of code found online or give up on the picky syntax and obscure rules.

This is an enormous problem for learners, particularly children. Why should one's imagination be confined to what may be Googled? If you can invent a physical artifact, "brick-by-brick" through tinkering, you should be able to do the same with the program you write to control your creation. There is much to be learned by reading another person's program/code and modifying it, but that should not be the only path to programming or physical computing. Imagine teaching writing by giving students twenty different words and telling them that their storytelling must be limited to only those words.

Today, the micro:bit is taking K-12 education by storm, not just because it is inexpensive, but because it is programmable by anyone. That is because the micro:bit was designed for the education sector and its developers took software seriously. Software is the nervous system of physical computing. Great hardware and the software powering it should be generative. "Messing about" with the micro:bit and the programming environments discussed in this book should generate project ideas. Each success generates other ideas. Bugs invite debugging.

The micro:bit is special

My recent book, *Twenty Things to Do with a Computer – Forward 50*, (Stager, 2021) celebrates the remarkable 1971 paper by Seymour Papert and Cynthia Solomon in which they provide a vision for how children may learn into the future (Papert & Solomon, 1971). More than fifty years ago, Papert and Solomon described the sorts of physical computing projects featured in this book. The variable that made such learning experiences rare for a half century of school children is the cost of hardware.

The micro:bit represents this paradigm shift in access and affordability. It is sufficiently powerful and flexible to meet the needs of learners and create opportunities beyond the limits of our imagination. It may just be that rarest of educational technology unicorn.

The micro:bit ticks several important boxes for educators. It's inexpensive and versatile—approximately $15, with a USB cable, battery box, and batteries. The micro:bit also works with Macs, PCs, Chromebooks, iOS, and Android devices. Paired with MakeCode, a free programming language, it is sufficiently powerful and flexible to meet the needs of learners and create opportunities beyond the limits of our imagination.

For many reasons, the micro:bit may be the physical computing platform of choice in schools for the next decade.

Go for it!

Since the micro:bit is a chip as cheap as chips, educators are more inclined to allow kids to use them in a daring fashion. Use one to learn coding, embed one in a robot, use another to control that robot remotely. Sew a micro:bit into your interactive garment, control a classroom puppet theatre with a pile of them, build a school weather station, or invent something new.

The BBC micro:bit, MakeCode, and this book combine to fuel remarkable ingenuity and powerful ideas for young people. We can't wait to see what teachers and students do with these remarkable resources!

Veteran teacher educator, Gary Stager, Ph.D., is president of Constructing Modern Knowledge Press, the publisher of The Invent to Learn Guide to the micro:bit.

References

Papert, S. (1980). *Mindstorms: children, computers, and powerful ideas.* Basic Books.

Papert, S., & Solomon, C. (1971). *Twenty things to do with a computer* (Artificial Intelligence Memo # 248, Issue.

Stager, G. (Ed.). (2021). *Twenty things to do with a computer forward 50: Future visions of education inspired by Seymour Papert and Cynthia Solomon's seminal work.* Constructing Modern Knowledge Press.

Material Gallery

Inventing with the micro:bit will be more fun and convenient if you collect tools and materials to enhance your projects. You may already have some of these items in your school or around your house.

Electrical Material

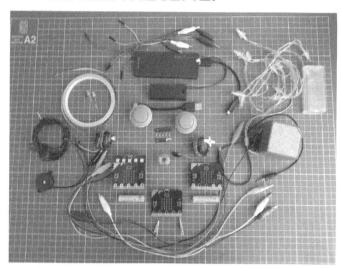

USB cables
Battery pack
Alligator clips and cables
LED lights
Christmas light strands
Conductive tape
ADA fruit LED sequins
Conductive thread
Rechargeable batteries
Game buttons
micro:bit add-on board
Servo motors (180 & 360)
Additional cables and connectors

Tools

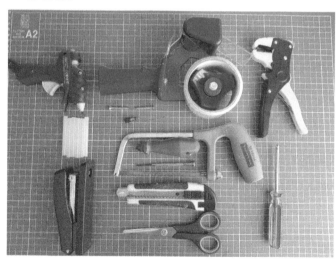

Scissors
Screwdrivers
Needle
Sharp pins
Wire stripper
Hot glue gun & glue sticks
Cutting knife
Box cutter
Hand saw
Tape
Stapler

Craft Material

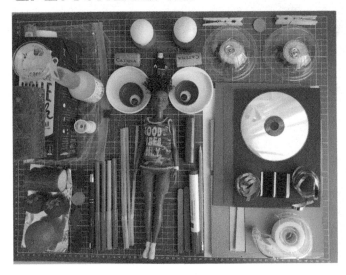

Cardboard

A variety of paper

Pencils, pens, markers

Felt & cloth

Foil

Tape & glue

Snaps & buttons

Velcro

Ping pong balls, googly eyes, decor items

Coins

Wooden sticks & dowels

Dolls, toys, stuffed animals

String, yarn, thread

Clothespins

Cups, drink lids, straws

CD

Sound

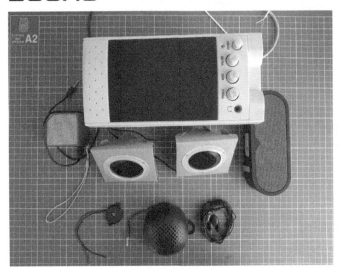

Headphones & earphones

USB powered speakers with a head jack

Old computer speaker

Piezo (small speaker)

Battery powered speakers with a head jack

About the Authors

Peter Heldens and Pauline Maas met in the summer of 2016 and immediately started to work together, combining Peter's technical know-how and Pauline's creative approach. After a year, the plan came together to make an online website with 101 projects for the micro:bit (microbit101.nl).

Since then, they have given hundreds of workshops and masterclasses to refine and try out the projects. The projects chosen for this book are the ones that work best in group situations, and build skills both in hardware and software.

Pauline Maas

After her studies (Textile and Dutch educator) in Delft, Pauline worked in Information Technology (ICT) at a variety of companies, learning on the job, and often as the only woman employed in ICT. After twenty years she decided that "If I want more female colleagues, I have to teach them." She started her own company 4PIP, teaching ICT and technology in schools and giving workshops for teachers. She noticed that there were not many coding books for children, and in 2008, her first book about GameMaker was published. More books followed about coding and how to implement coding in your school (*CodeKlas*). Since 2018 she has been the EU Coding Ambassador and is organizing CodeWeek in The Netherlands.

Two days a week she is an ICT teacher at Royal Visio (a school for visually impaired students where she is implementing the Coding Curriculum). The rest of the week she is writing, giving lectures and workshops, and having fun with making lots and lots of projects.

For her, the micro:bit is the best way to implement computational thinking at schools and is the perfect way for people of all ages to make, invent, learn, code, solve problems, work together, persevere—and have fun!

Peter Heldens

Peter graduated in 1993 with a MScs in Computing Science and has been working at Microsoft since 2007. In his spare time, he delivers Innovation workshops inspiring participants to build gadgets and Internet of Things (IoT) devices. Leveraging open-source software and hardware, 3D design, 3D printing, and microcontrollers, he teaches everyone from 8 to 80 how to innovate!

In early 2010, Peter developed a conference call app with TouchDevelop (an experimental programming language developed by Microsoft Research). When his app went viral, he met Peli de Halleux, lead developer of TouchDevelop, the predecessor of what later evolved into MakeCode.

Peter's life changed significantly after he received one of the first micro:bits from Peli in 2014. This enabled Peter to innovate much faster, creating even more cool projects in his workshop, such as high-pressure baseball machines, hockey games, NeoPixels attached to skis to teach parallel skiing, Milky Monsters, and many others. For more projects, see @peterheldens on Twitter.

Once Peter met Pauline in the summer of 2016, they created over 100 micro:bit projects, published on microbit101.nl website. In 2019 they presented the craziest projects at the BBC microbit:live event in Manchester. Many of these projects were the start of this book.

Let this book be the start of your innovation journey. The only limitation is your own inspiration!

Illustrator

Angelique Krijnen is a professional botanical artist. She contributed the unique illustrations for this book, drawing first in pen and filling them in with watercolors. (angeliquekrijnen.nl)

Also From Constructing Modern Knowledge Press

Constructing Modern Knowledge Press publishes books for modern learning. See more at cmkpress.com.

Invent to Learn: Making, Tinkering, and Engineering in the Classroom
by Sylvia Libow Martinez and Gary S. Stager

An all new and expanded edition of the book called "the bible of the Maker Movement in classrooms," *Invent to Learn* has become the most popular book for educators seeking to understand how modern tools and technology can revolutionize education.

Learning to Code – An Invitation to Computer Science Through the Art and Patterns of Nature (Snap! or Lynx Editions)
by David Thornburg

These are books about discovery—the discoveries each of us can make when finding beauty in geometric patterns, beauty in mathematics, and beauty in computer programming. This is also a guide for teaching children to program computers in uniquely powerful ways.

Available in either a Lynx or Snap! edition—two powerful programming languages designed for learning.

20 Things to Do with a Computer Forward 50: Future Visions of Education Inspired by Seymour Papert and Cynthia Solomon's Seminal Work

edited by Gary S. Stager, foreword by Cynthia Solomon

In 1971, Cynthia Solomon and Seymour Papert published *Twenty Things to Do with a Computer*, a revolutionary document that would set the course of education for the next fifty years and beyond. This book is a celebration of the vision set forth by Papert and Solomon a half-century ago. Four dozen experts from around the world invite us to consider the original provocations, reflect on their implementation, and chart a course for the future through personal recollections, learning stories, and imaginative scenarios.

The Art of Digital Fabrication: STEAM Projects for the Makerspace and Art Studio

by Erin E. Riley

Integrate STEAM in your school through arts-based maker projects using digital fabrication tools commonly found in makerspaces like 3D printers, laser cutters, vinyl cutters, and CNC machines. Full color pages showcase the artistic and technical work of students that results from combining art with engineering and design. Written by an educator with experience in art and maker education, this volume contains over twenty-five makerspace tested projects, a material and process inventory for digital fabrication, guides for designing with software, and how-tos for using digital fabrication machines.

Scrappy Circuits

by Michael Carroll

The best dollar you'll ever spend on a child's STEAM education! Scrappy Circuits is an imaginative "do-it-yourself" way to learn about electrical circuits for less than $1 per person. Raid your junk drawer for simple office supplies, add a little cardboard, pay a visit to a local dollar store, and you are on your way to countless fun projects for learning about electronics.

The Invent to Learn Guide to Fun

by Josh Burker

The Invent to Learn Guide to Fun features an assortment of insanely clever classroom-tested maker projects for learners of all ages. Josh Burker kicks classroom learning-by-making up a notch with step-by-step instructions, full-color photos, open-ended challenges, and sample code. Learn to paint with light, make your own Operation Game, sew interactive stuffed creatures, build Rube Goldberg machines, design artbots, produce mathematically generated mosaic tiles, program adventure games, and more!

The Invent to Learn Guide to MORE FUN

by Josh Burker

Josh Burker is back with a second volume of all new projects for learners who just want MORE! Insanely clever classroom-tested "maker" projects for learners of all ages with coding, microcontrollers, 3D printing, LEGO machines, and more! The projects feature step-by-step instructions and full-color photos.

The Invent to Learn Guide to Making in the K-3 Classroom: Why, How, and Wow!

by Alice Baggett

This full color book packed with photos is a practical guide for primary school educators who want to inspire their students to embrace a tinkering mindset so they can invent fantastic contraptions. Veteran teacher Alice Baggett shares her expertise in how to create hands-on learning experiences for young inventors so students experience the thrilling process of making—complete with epic fails and spectacular discoveries.

The Invent to Learn Guide to 3D Printing in the Classroom: Recipes for Success

by David Thornburg, Norma Thornburg, and Sara Armstrong

This book is an essential guide for educators interested in bringing the amazing world of 3D printing to their classrooms. Eighteen fun and challenging projects explore science, technology, engineering, and mathematics, along with forays into the visual arts and design.

Meaningful Making: Projects and Inspirations for Fab Labs & Makerspaces (Volumes 1 & 2)

Edited by Paulo Blikstein, Sylvia Libow Martinez, Heather Allen Pang

Project ideas, articles, best practices, and assessment strategies from educators at the forefront of making and hands-on, minds-on education. In these two volumes, FabLearn Fellows share inspirational ideas from their learning spaces, assessment strategies and recommended projects across a broad range of age levels. Illustrated with color photos of real student work, the Fellows take you on a tour of the future of learning, where children make sense of the world by making things that matter to them and their communities.

Making Science: Reimagining STEM Education in Middle School and Beyond

by Christa Flores

Anthropologist turned science and making teacher Christa Flores shares her classroom tested lessons and resources for learning by making and design in the middle grades and beyond. Richly illustrated with examples of student work, this book offers project ideas, connections to the Next Generation Science Standards, assessment strategies, and practical tips for educators.

The Inner Principal: Reflections on Educational Leadership

by David Loader

"This is a book that will go to your inner consciousness and make a difference in how you think about your own role as leader." – from the foreword by Michael Fullan

Education Outrage

by Roger C. Schank

Roger Schank has had it with the stupid, lazy, greedy, cynical, and uninformed forces setting outrageous education policy, wrecking childhood, and preparing students for a world that will never exist. The short essays in this book will make you mad, sad, argue with your friends, and take action.